Preparing Students for
Standardized Testing

Grade 3

By
JANET P. SITTER, Ph.D.

COPYRIGHT © 2004 Mark Twain Media, Inc.

ISBN 13-digit: 978-1-58037-265-7
10-digit: 1-58037-265-1

Printing No. CD-1625

Mark Twain Media, Inc., Publishers
Distributed by Carson-Dellosa Publishing LLC

Visit us at www.carsondellosa.com

Table of Contents

Introduction iv
Content Area Skills v
The Language of Tests viii
Overview of Testing Tips x
Filling Out the Answer Sheet xi

Test Lessons:

Unit One: Reading: Helpful Reading Strategies 1
  Lesson One: Vocabulary: synonyms, antonyms, words in context, multiple meanings, classification 2
  Lesson Two: Word Analysis: prefixes, suffixes, root words, contractions, homophones 8
  Lesson Three: Reading Comprehension: main idea/supporting details; inferring relationships; cause/effect, fact/opinion; identifying theme and story elements, character traits 12

Unit Two: Language: Helpful Language Strategies 20
  Lesson One: Mechanics: punctuation, capitalization, spelling, usage 21
  Lesson Two: Expression: topic sentences/supporting details, concluding sentences, connective/transitional words and phrases, sequence of ideas 30
  Lesson Three: Information Skills: using references (resource books, telephone directory, dictionary); interpreting data from charts and graphs; using computer resources 39

Unit Three: Mathematics: Helpful Math Strategies 47
  Lesson One: Concepts: number and operations, patterns, relationships, algebra, geometry, measurement, data, probability 48
  Lesson Two: Computation: addition, subtraction, multiplication, division, whole numbers, decimals, fractions, percent 58
  Lesson Three: Problem Solving and Reasoning: problem solving; patterns and relationships; inductive/deductive reasoning; relating models, diagrams, and pictures to math ideas, estimation 63

Table of Contents (cont.)

Unit Four: Science: Helpful Science Strategies... **69**
    Lesson One: Process and Inquiry: scientific process, interpret data, draw
        conclusions, predict events... 70
    Lesson Two: Concepts: animals, weather, health, human body 75

Unit Five: Social Studies: Helpful Social Studies Strategies **85**
    Lesson One: History and Culture: customs, norms, and social institutions
        through a multicultural perspective; leaders, main events, symbols, broad
        themes, and trends in U.S. and world history 86
    Lesson Two: Civics, Government, and Economics: structure, function, and
        purposes of government; rights and responsibilities of citizens; producers,
        consumers, goods, and services 91
    Lesson Three: Geography: maps, globes, geographic terms, land forms,
        weather and climate 97

Practice Answer Sheets... 106
Answer Keys 111

Introduction

Standardized tests are designed to measure how well a student has learned the basic knowledge and skills that are taught in elementary and middle schools. They generally cover the content areas of reading, vocabulary, language, spelling, math, science, and social studies. The most recent standardized tests also focus on the student's ability to think critically. It would be unrealistic, however, to expect that students will know (or have been taught) all of the material on the tests. Some of this material will be new to students, and this may cause anxiety in both students and teachers.

The purpose of this book is to help you familiarize your students with the format and language of tests, with important test-taking strategies, and with practice in the content areas of the major standardized tests used nationally. These include:

- **The California Achievement Tests (CAT/5)**

- **The Iowa Tests of Basic Skills (ITBS)**

- **The Comprehensive Tests of Basic Skills (CTBS)**

- **The Stanford Achievement Tests (SAT)**

- **The Metropolitan Achievement Tests (MAT)**

- **The Texas Assessment of Knowledge and Skills (TAKS)**

By spending 20 minutes a day for three weeks prior to the administration of the standardized test for your school district and grade level and using the material in this book, you will not only increase your students' confidence in their test-taking skills but also help them to successfully demonstrate their knowledge and skills. *Preparing Students for Standardized Testing* will provide your students with opportunities to take practice tests under similar conditions to those that exist on standardized tests. Teachers should photocopy the practice tests in the book and the practice answer sheets for students to use. This will familiarize students with the process of filling in computer-scored answer sheets. In order to better prepare your students for standardized testing, it may be beneficial to set a time limit you think is appropriate for the average student in your class.

Content Area Skills

<u>READING</u>

Word Analysis:
✔ Identify prefixes, suffixes, root words
✔ Recognize contractions
✔ Demonstrate knowledge of sound/symbol and structural relationships in letters, words, signs

Vocabulary:
✔ Identify synonyms, antonyms, homonyms
✔ Recognize word meaning and words in context
✔ Demonstrate knowledge of multiple meanings of words

Comprehension:
✔ Identify main idea and supporting details
✔ Recognize theme, story elements, genre, author's purpose, and use of figurative language
✔ Demonstrate literal/interpretive understanding
✔ Distinguish fact/opinion, cause/effect, reality/fantasy
✔ Demonstrate critical understanding by drawing conclusions, making predictions, and extending meaning to other contexts

<u>LANGUAGE</u>

Mechanics:
✔ Identify the appropriate use of capitalization, punctuation, and parts of speech in text
✔ Recognize correct spelling in text
✔ Identify misspelled words in text

Expression:
✔ Identify topic, concluding, and supporting sentences in text
✔ Determine correct usage, sequence of ideas, and relevance of information
✔ Recognize connective/transitional words, phrases, and sentences
✔ Identify and correct errors in existing text and in text written by student

Information Skills:
✔ Identify parts of a book
✔ Recognize and use a dictionary and other reference materials
✔ Demonstrate the ability to understand and interpret maps, charts, and diagrams

Content Area Skills (cont.)

<u>MATHEMATICS</u>

Concepts:
✔ Identify, compare, and order numbers and number operations
✔ Recognize and compare equivalent numbers
✔ Interpret and apply numbers in real-world situations

Computation:
✔ Identify the properties and relationships of numbers and operations
✔ Recognize and extend patterns, transformations, symmetry, and geometric figures
✔ Recognize and solve real-world computation problems
✔ Demonstrate proficiency in computation procedures in addition, subtraction, multiplication, and division

Problem Solving and Reasoning:
✔ Identify and apply problem-solving strategies to real-world problems
✔ Recognize and interpret data in models, diagrams, pictures, graphs
✔ Use a variety of estimation strategies; determine reasonableness of results
✔ Demonstrate inductive/deductive reasoning and spatial and proportional reasoning to solve real-world problems

<u>SCIENCE</u>

Process and Inquiry:
✔ Identify scientific principles, processes, and inquiry
✔ Interpret and make reasonable interpretations from scientific data
✔ Recognize use of inferences to draw conclusions
✔ Demonstrate an understanding of fundamental concepts of scientific inquiry

Concepts:
✔ Identify characteristics of plants/animals, energy systems, solutions/mixtures
✔ Recognize basic principles of Earth and space
✔ Demonstrate knowledge of basic health and nutrition for the human body

Content Area Skills (cont.)

SOCIAL STUDIES

History and Cultures:
- ✔ Identify certain famous people, holidays, symbols, customs, norms, and social institutions
- ✔ Recognize the contributions, influences, and interactions of various cultures
- ✔ Demonstrate a historical understanding of time, continuity, and societal change in the United States and the world

Civics and Government:
- ✔ Identify government bodies and characteristics of good citizenship
- ✔ Recognize consequences of responsible and irresponsible behavior in government
- ✔ Demonstrate an understanding of the structure, function, and purpose of government

Economics:
- ✔ Identify economic principles of supply/demand, consumer/producer, goods/services, profit/loss
- ✔ Recognize three roles individuals play: worker, consumer, citizen
- ✔ Demonstrate an understanding of how the general social/political/economic environment affects opportunity and happiness

Geography:
- ✔ Identify and use geographic terms to describe land forms, bodies of water, weather, and climate
- ✔ Recognize how human use of the environment is influenced by cultural values, economic wants, level of technology, and environmental perceptions
- ✔ Demonstrate geographic methods to interpret maps, graphs, charts, and photographs

The Language of Tests

Here are some of the most frequently used terms in assessment.

Accountability: The practice of evaluating teachers and schools, based on measurable goals

Achievement Test: Tests designed to measure knowledge and skills, usually objective, standardized, and norm-referenced

Alternative Assessment: Methods of evaluating student work and progress that are *not* traditional standardized tests (e.g., portfolios, anecdotal records, teacher observation, interviews, performance, demonstration projects, etc.)

Assessment: A systematic method for testing student progress and achievement

Authentic Assessment: The tasks and procedures used for assessment are closely related to tasks found in the real world.

Content Validity: The extent to which the content of a test actually measures the knowledge and skills the test claims to measure

Criterion-referenced Test: A test that measures a student's performance to a predetermined measure of success rather than to a norm group

Curricular Validity: The extent to which a test measures what has been taught

Diagnostic Test: A test used to assess specific characteristics in order to make instructional decisions

Evaluation: The process of making judgments and instructional decisions obtained from a form of assessment

Grade Equivalent Score: A measure that compares a student's raw score on a standardized test to average scores across grade levels

Group Test: A test that is administered to more than one student at the same time

Individual Test: A test that is administered to only one student at a time

Intelligence Test: A test that measures a student's general mental ability or scholastic aptitude

Mean: The average of a set of test scores

Median: The middle score of a set of test scores

The Language of Tests (cont.)

Minimum-competency Test: A test that measures whether a student has attained the minimum level of overall achievement necessary for a particular purpose

Mode: The most frequent score of a group of scores

National Standards: A set of standards for an entire country, usually including content standards, performance standards, and school standards

Norm Group: The group whose test performance is used to establish levels of performance on a standardized test.

Norm-referenced Test: Test that measures the student's score with the average performance of all test-takers

Objective Test: Test in which each question is stated in such a way that there is only one correct answer

Percentage Score: The percentage of correct responses on a test

Percentile Score: Proportion of other students' scores that equal or fall below a given student's score

Population: A complete set of students to which a set of test results will be generalized

Portfolio Assessment: Collecting children's work on an ongoing basis and examining it for evidence of growth

Raw Score: The number of correct responses on a test

Reliability: The consistency in test results or the degree to which a test's results actually measure what a student can do

Standardized Test: A test with specific procedures such that comparable measures may be made by testers in different geographic areas

Test Bias: Tendency for a test to be unfair for students in some groups but not in others

Validity: The degree to which a test measures what it is designed to measure

Writing Assessment: A test in which students are asked to demonstrate writing abilities by actually writing in response to given prompts

Overview of Testing Tips

- Read (or listen) to directions carefully.

- Follow all instructions, including icons.

- Read the entire question.

- Read all answer choices before picking one.

- Budget your time wisely.

- Do not spend too much time on any one question.

- Use all of the time provided; testing is not the same as a race.

- Pay close attention to how the question is worded.

- Avoid making answer sheet errors.

- Skip hard questions, and answer the easy ones first.

- Use the process of elimination to find answers.

- Use logical reasoning to choose the best answer.

- When all else fails, guess!

- Answer all test questions.

- Think twice before changing an answer.

- Control test anxiety.

- Stay calm and focus on the task at hand.

Hi! Look for me. Whenever you see me, I'll give you a testing tip to help with your test-taking skills.

Filling Out the Answer Sheet

The first thing you will do during standardized testing is to correctly fill out your answer sheet. Below is an example of an answer sheet. The circles must be filled in for every box, so for empty boxes, fill in the empty circles. Use a No. 2 pencil so the computer can score your answer sheet. Fill in your circles completely, and fill in only one for each question. If you erase an answer, be sure that you erase completely before filling in your new choice. The computer will mark wrong any question that seems to have more than one choice marked. Erase all stray pencil marks on the page.

Practice filling out this sample form with your name. Print your name in the boxes at the top. Then darken the circle for that letter in the column under each letter. For blank spaces, darken the blank circles.

STUDENT'S NAME

Last												First							M.I.
○	○	○	○	○	○	○	○	○	○	○	○	○	○	○	○	○	○	○	○
Ⓐ	Ⓐ	Ⓐ	Ⓐ	Ⓐ	Ⓐ	Ⓐ	Ⓐ	Ⓐ	Ⓐ	Ⓐ	Ⓐ	Ⓐ	Ⓐ	Ⓐ	Ⓐ	Ⓐ	Ⓐ	Ⓐ	Ⓐ
Ⓑ	Ⓑ	Ⓑ	Ⓑ	Ⓑ	Ⓑ	Ⓑ	Ⓑ	Ⓑ	Ⓑ	Ⓑ	Ⓑ	Ⓑ	Ⓑ	Ⓑ	Ⓑ	Ⓑ	Ⓑ	Ⓑ	Ⓑ
Ⓒ	Ⓒ	Ⓒ	Ⓒ	Ⓒ	Ⓒ	Ⓒ	Ⓒ	Ⓒ	Ⓒ	Ⓒ	Ⓒ	Ⓒ	Ⓒ	Ⓒ	Ⓒ	Ⓒ	Ⓒ	Ⓒ	Ⓒ
Ⓓ	Ⓓ	Ⓓ	Ⓓ	Ⓓ	Ⓓ	Ⓓ	Ⓓ	Ⓓ	Ⓓ	Ⓓ	Ⓓ	Ⓓ	Ⓓ	Ⓓ	Ⓓ	Ⓓ	Ⓓ	Ⓓ	Ⓓ
Ⓔ	Ⓔ	Ⓔ	Ⓔ	Ⓔ	Ⓔ	Ⓔ	Ⓔ	Ⓔ	Ⓔ	Ⓔ	Ⓔ	Ⓔ	Ⓔ	Ⓔ	Ⓔ	Ⓔ	Ⓔ	Ⓔ	Ⓔ
Ⓕ	Ⓕ	Ⓕ	Ⓕ	Ⓕ	Ⓕ	Ⓕ	Ⓕ	Ⓕ	Ⓕ	Ⓕ	Ⓕ	Ⓕ	Ⓕ	Ⓕ	Ⓕ	Ⓕ	Ⓕ	Ⓕ	Ⓕ
Ⓖ	Ⓖ	Ⓖ	Ⓖ	Ⓖ	Ⓖ	Ⓖ	Ⓖ	Ⓖ	Ⓖ	Ⓖ	Ⓖ	Ⓖ	Ⓖ	Ⓖ	Ⓖ	Ⓖ	Ⓖ	Ⓖ	Ⓖ
Ⓗ	Ⓗ	Ⓗ	Ⓗ	Ⓗ	Ⓗ	Ⓗ	Ⓗ	Ⓗ	Ⓗ	Ⓗ	Ⓗ	Ⓗ	Ⓗ	Ⓗ	Ⓗ	Ⓗ	Ⓗ	Ⓗ	Ⓗ
Ⓘ	Ⓘ	Ⓘ	Ⓘ	Ⓘ	Ⓘ	Ⓘ	Ⓘ	Ⓘ	Ⓘ	Ⓘ	Ⓘ	Ⓘ	Ⓘ	Ⓘ	Ⓘ	Ⓘ	Ⓘ	Ⓘ	Ⓘ
Ⓙ	Ⓙ	Ⓙ	Ⓙ	Ⓙ	Ⓙ	Ⓙ	Ⓙ	Ⓙ	Ⓙ	Ⓙ	Ⓙ	Ⓙ	Ⓙ	Ⓙ	Ⓙ	Ⓙ	Ⓙ	Ⓙ	Ⓙ
Ⓚ	Ⓚ	Ⓚ	Ⓚ	Ⓚ	Ⓚ	Ⓚ	Ⓚ	Ⓚ	Ⓚ	Ⓚ	Ⓚ	Ⓚ	Ⓚ	Ⓚ	Ⓚ	Ⓚ	Ⓚ	Ⓚ	Ⓚ
Ⓛ	Ⓛ	Ⓛ	Ⓛ	Ⓛ	Ⓛ	Ⓛ	Ⓛ	Ⓛ	Ⓛ	Ⓛ	Ⓛ	Ⓛ	Ⓛ	Ⓛ	Ⓛ	Ⓛ	Ⓛ	Ⓛ	Ⓛ
Ⓜ	Ⓜ	Ⓜ	Ⓜ	Ⓜ	Ⓜ	Ⓜ	Ⓜ	Ⓜ	Ⓜ	Ⓜ	Ⓜ	Ⓜ	Ⓜ	Ⓜ	Ⓜ	Ⓜ	Ⓜ	Ⓜ	Ⓜ
Ⓝ	Ⓝ	Ⓝ	Ⓝ	Ⓝ	Ⓝ	Ⓝ	Ⓝ	Ⓝ	Ⓝ	Ⓝ	Ⓝ	Ⓝ	Ⓝ	Ⓝ	Ⓝ	Ⓝ	Ⓝ	Ⓝ	Ⓝ
Ⓞ	Ⓞ	Ⓞ	Ⓞ	Ⓞ	Ⓞ	Ⓞ	Ⓞ	Ⓞ	Ⓞ	Ⓞ	Ⓞ	Ⓞ	Ⓞ	Ⓞ	Ⓞ	Ⓞ	Ⓞ	Ⓞ	Ⓞ
Ⓟ	Ⓟ	Ⓟ	Ⓟ	Ⓟ	Ⓟ	Ⓟ	Ⓟ	Ⓟ	Ⓟ	Ⓟ	Ⓟ	Ⓟ	Ⓟ	Ⓟ	Ⓟ	Ⓟ	Ⓟ	Ⓟ	Ⓟ
Ⓠ	Ⓠ	Ⓠ	Ⓠ	Ⓠ	Ⓠ	Ⓠ	Ⓠ	Ⓠ	Ⓠ	Ⓠ	Ⓠ	Ⓠ	Ⓠ	Ⓠ	Ⓠ	Ⓠ	Ⓠ	Ⓠ	Ⓠ
Ⓡ	Ⓡ	Ⓡ	Ⓡ	Ⓡ	Ⓡ	Ⓡ	Ⓡ	Ⓡ	Ⓡ	Ⓡ	Ⓡ	Ⓡ	Ⓡ	Ⓡ	Ⓡ	Ⓡ	Ⓡ	Ⓡ	Ⓡ
Ⓢ	Ⓢ	Ⓢ	Ⓢ	Ⓢ	Ⓢ	Ⓢ	Ⓢ	Ⓢ	Ⓢ	Ⓢ	Ⓢ	Ⓢ	Ⓢ	Ⓢ	Ⓢ	Ⓢ	Ⓢ	Ⓢ	Ⓢ
Ⓣ	Ⓣ	Ⓣ	Ⓣ	Ⓣ	Ⓣ	Ⓣ	Ⓣ	Ⓣ	Ⓣ	Ⓣ	Ⓣ	Ⓣ	Ⓣ	Ⓣ	Ⓣ	Ⓣ	Ⓣ	Ⓣ	Ⓣ
Ⓤ	Ⓤ	Ⓤ	Ⓤ	Ⓤ	Ⓤ	Ⓤ	Ⓤ	Ⓤ	Ⓤ	Ⓤ	Ⓤ	Ⓤ	Ⓤ	Ⓤ	Ⓤ	Ⓤ	Ⓤ	Ⓤ	Ⓤ
Ⓥ	Ⓥ	Ⓥ	Ⓥ	Ⓥ	Ⓥ	Ⓥ	Ⓥ	Ⓥ	Ⓥ	Ⓥ	Ⓥ	Ⓥ	Ⓥ	Ⓥ	Ⓥ	Ⓥ	Ⓥ	Ⓥ	Ⓥ
Ⓦ	Ⓦ	Ⓦ	Ⓦ	Ⓦ	Ⓦ	Ⓦ	Ⓦ	Ⓦ	Ⓦ	Ⓦ	Ⓦ	Ⓦ	Ⓦ	Ⓦ	Ⓦ	Ⓦ	Ⓦ	Ⓦ	Ⓦ
Ⓧ	Ⓧ	Ⓧ	Ⓧ	Ⓧ	Ⓧ	Ⓧ	Ⓧ	Ⓧ	Ⓧ	Ⓧ	Ⓧ	Ⓧ	Ⓧ	Ⓧ	Ⓧ	Ⓧ	Ⓧ	Ⓧ	Ⓧ
Ⓨ	Ⓨ	Ⓨ	Ⓨ	Ⓨ	Ⓨ	Ⓨ	Ⓨ	Ⓨ	Ⓨ	Ⓨ	Ⓨ	Ⓨ	Ⓨ	Ⓨ	Ⓨ	Ⓨ	Ⓨ	Ⓨ	Ⓨ
Ⓩ	Ⓩ	Ⓩ	Ⓩ	Ⓩ	Ⓩ	Ⓩ	Ⓩ	Ⓩ	Ⓩ	Ⓩ	Ⓩ	Ⓩ	Ⓩ	Ⓩ	Ⓩ	Ⓩ	Ⓩ	Ⓩ	Ⓩ

Filling Out the Answer Sheet (cont.)

Practice filling out this sample form with your birth date, gender, and grade. Print your teacher's name, school name, and district in the boxes at the top. Then darken the circles for your birth date, gender, and grade.

TEACHER		
SCHOOL		
DISTRICT		

BIRTH DATE

Month	Day	Year
Jan ○	⓪ ⓪	⓪ ⓪
Feb ○	① ①	① ①
Mar ○	② ②	② ②
Apr ○	③ ③	③ ③
May ○	④	④ ④
Jun ○	⑤	⑤ ⑤
Jul ○	⑥	⑥ ⑥
Aug ○	⑦	⑦ ⑦
Sep ○	⑧	⑧ ⑧
Oct ○	⑨	⑨ ⑨
Nov ○		
Dec ○		

GENDER

○ Female   ○ Male

GRADE

Ⓚ   ①   ②   ③   ④   ⑤

Name: _____　Date: _____

Lesson One: Vocabulary (cont.)

Directions: For items #23–30, read the story. For each of the blanks, there is a list of words with the same number. Choose the word from each list that <u>best completes</u> the meaning of the story.

Deaf people talk in many ways. Some learn to use their ___23___, while others learn to talk by using their ___24___ in a special sign language.

23. A.　talents　　　　C.　hands
　　B.　voices　　　　D.　ears

24. A.　hands　　　　C.　ears
　　B.　voices　　　　D.　talents

Barney has a(n) ___25___ message for you. You must read it ___26___.

25. A.　happy　　　　C.　urgent
　　B.　birthday　　　D.　secret

26. A.　soon　　　　C.　slowly
　　B.　immediately　D.　carefully

The monster movie ___27___ Gail. Her brother Gabe was ___28___ too.

27. A.　bored　　　　C.　terrified
　　B.　amused　　　D.　tired

28. A.　frightened　　C.　happy
　　B.　bored　　　　D.　delighted

I had a terrible ___29___ last night. This ___30___ woke me up.

29. A.　stomachache　C.　time
　　B.　vision　　　　D.　dream

30. A.　scream　　　C.　plan
　　B.　nightmare　　D.　ghost

Name: _____   Date: _____

Lesson One: Vocabulary (cont.)

We had a very bad __31__ last night. The wind knocked down __32__ and blew __33__ into buildings. It was really __34__. We thought it might be a __35__.

31. A. rain   C. dream
    B. storm   D. dinner

32. A. people   C. ghosts
    B. trees   D. monkeys

33. A. fish   C. cars
    B. trains   D. leaves

34. A. big   C. scary
    B. long   D. cool

35. A. hurricane C. monsoon
    B. tornado   D. rainbow

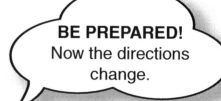

BE QUICK!
The format changes again … into a paragraph.

Directions: For items #36–38, choose the word from the answer choices that goes with the three words in the item.

---

36. roses, pansies, daisies
    A. cherries   C. apples
    B. daffodils   D. coins

37. red, green, purple
    A. blocks   C. brown
    B. cards   D. baseball

38. stone, sand, rock
    A. camel   C. grass
    B. boulder   D. tree

BE PREPARED!
Now the directions change.

Name: _____ Date: _____

Lesson One: Vocabulary (cont.)

Directions: Choose the word that tells about the underlined word.

39. <u>monkey</u>
    A.   deep
    B.   cool
    C.   silly
    D.   wide

40. <u>house</u>
    A.   cluttered
    B.   clever
    C.   speedy
    D.   tired

BE HAPPY! You are done with Lesson One.

Review

1. Read <u>all</u> directions carefully.
2. Be sure you understand the directions.
3. Read all answer choices before choosing one.
4. Format changes do <u>not</u> always signal a change in directions.

Name: _____   Date: _____

UNIT ONE: READING

Lesson Two: Word Analysis

BE SHARP!
What is the key word in the directions? Circle it.

Directions:
This is a test of words and their parts. For items #1–5, read each word carefully. Then choose the word that has the root word underlined.

1. A. swi<u>mm</u>ing
    B. lo<u>ne</u>ly
    C. <u>happ</u>iness
    D. cheer<u>ful</u>

2. A. <u>cra</u>zy
    B. per<u>mit</u>
    C. <u>sad</u>ness
    D. toma<u>toes</u>

3. A. <u> purple</u>
    B. can<u>dle</u>
    C. <u> pianos</u>
    D. <u> doctor</u>

4. A. some<u>one</u>
    B. in<u>ches</u>
    C. <u>wind</u>y
    D. ligh<u>tning</u>

5. A. un<u>happ</u>y
    B. hope<u>ful</u>
    C. <u>en</u>couragement
    D. <u>cheer</u>ful

BE SMART!
What are you looking for in items #6–10?

Directions:
For items #6–10, read each word carefully. Choose the word that has the suffix underlined.

6. A. <u>sick</u>
    B. sick<u>ly</u>
    C. <u>sick</u>ness
    D. <u>un</u>sick

7. A. <u>play</u>
    B. pla<u>ying</u>
    C. play<u>ful</u>
    D. <u>re</u>play

Name: _____ Date: _____

Lesson Two: Word Analysis (cont.)

8. A. friend<u>ly</u>   B. <u>friend</u>   C. <u>un</u>friendly   D. fr<u>iend</u>ship

9. A. <u>safe</u>   B. <u>un</u>safe   C. safe<u>ty</u>   D. <u>safe</u>ly

10. A. <u>soft</u>ness   B. soft<u>ly</u>   C. <u>soft</u>   D. <u>soft</u>est

BE AWARE!
Changes in format <u>do</u> <u>not</u> always mean a change in directions.

11. A. sparkle
     B. whistle
     C. wrote
     D. sailboat

> **Directions:**
> For items #11–15, choose the word that is a compound word.

12. A. autumn
     B. broomstick
     C. taught
     D. comb

13. A. cereal
     B. orange
     C. oatmeal
     D. crumbs

14. A. sunburn
     B. escape
     C. camera
     D. skin

BE THOUGHTFUL!
Just what <u>is</u> a compound word?

15. A. enough
     B. Christmas
     C. birthday
     D. nickel

Name: _____ Date: _____

Lesson Two: Word Analysis (cont.)

16. I've
    A. I am
    B. I was
    C. I have
    D. I had

BE CLEVER!
Underline the key word or words in the directions.

17. haven't
    A. have went
    B. have not
    C. have got
    D. we have

18. She'll
    A. She will
    B. She won't
    C. She is
    D. She was

19. I'm
    A. I must
    B. I made
    C. I am
    D. I am not

20. you're
    A. your
    B. you will
    C. you won't
    D. you are

Name: _____ Date: _____

Lesson Three: Reading Comprehension (cont.)

This African-American folk tale was passed among slaves as they worked in the cotton fields of the South. The story was only recently written down. It goes something like this:

The People Could Fly

Long ago in Africa, it was said that people had wings and magic words that allowed them to fly. When the people were captured for slaves and put aboard the slaveships, there wasn't room for their wings, so they couldn't bring them along. There was, however, room for the magic words the people kept in their memories.

Slaves worked picking cotton from sunup to sundown. One hot, blistering, sunny day, the slaves had been working the cotton fields where it was so hot the sun singed the hair on their heads. Sarah, a young slave mother, carried her baby strapped on her back. She was so hot and so tired that she eventually fainted. This drew the quick but unwanted attention of the overseer. He rushed over to Sarah, who was crumpled in a heap, and cracked his whip cruelly across her back. "Back to work," the man snarled. All of the slaves were watching. Sarah struggled back to her feet and continued picking cotton. An old man known as Toby slowly began to inch his way over to where Sarah was picking, but before he could get there, she fell again. "Get up!" roared the overseer, again cracking his whip on Sarah's back, this time hurting Sarah's baby.

Sarah's baby cried out with the hurt; Sarah went down again. "Shut that thing up!" the overseer bellowed, raising his whip ready to strike. But before he could whip her again, the old man whispered "*Kum ... yali, kum buba tambe,*" and other magic words so quickly and softly that they sounded like the whispers and sighs of the wind.

Sarah began to rise up with her baby in her arms, feeling the magic of Africa. She rose up and up just like a bird, light as a feather. Up, up she went, flying over fields and woods; flying over the plantation house out of sight of the fields and the overseer. Like an eagle, she flew her way to freedom.

No one dared speak. No one could believe it. But they knew it was true, because they had seen it with their own eyes.

Name: _____ Date: _____

Lesson Three: Reading Comprehension (cont.)

Directions: Mark only the BEST answer for each multiple-choice question.

BE WATCHFUL! There may be more than one right answer.

11. Toby's actions
    A. helped Sarah fly back to Africa.
    B. helped the overseer to keep Sarah picking cotton.
    C. helped other slaves escape to freedom.
    D. helped Sarah escape the misery of the cottonfields.

12. In the second paragraph of the story, the author said, **"it was so hot the sun singed the hair on their heads."** What did the author mean by this?
    A. It was an extremely hot day.
    B. The day was so hot the slaves shaved their heads.
    C. It was so hot the slaves had to wear hats.
    D. It was so hot their hair burst into flame.

BE SURE to read all answers before you choose one.

13. How did the cruel overseer control the slaves?
    A. By whipping them
    B. By telling the master about them
    C. By yelling at them
    D. By hurting them

14. Why was Sarah in trouble with the overseer?
    A. Because she had to stop and quiet her baby
    B. Because she wasn't working hard enough
    C. Because she kept trying to escape
    D. Because she was upset for getting hit

15. In the last paragraph, the author said, **"No one dared speak."** What do you think was the reason for this?
    A. It was hard to believe what they had seen.
    B. They were afraid of being whipped themselves.
    C. No one saw exactly where Sarah went.
    D. Nobody except Toby knew the magic words.

Name: _____ Date: _____

UNIT TWO: LANGUAGE

Lesson One: Mechanics

Capitalization

Directions:

This is a test on capitalization. It will show how well you can use capital letters in sentences. Look for the sections that contain mistakes in capitalization in the sentences on this test. Some sentences do not have any mistakes.

---

1. A.   Daily exercise makes
   B.   you feel good
   C.   About yourself.
   D.   (no mistakes)

2. A.   exercise helps you think
   B.   better, sleep better, and
   C.   feel more relaxed.
   D.   (no mistakes)

3. A.   Regular exercise will
   B.   make you strong, like
   C.   venus williams.
   D.   (no mistakes)

4. A.   Exercise will also make
   B.   you better at physical
   C.   activities, like golf.
   D.   (no mistakes)

5. A.   tiger woods won
   B.   golf tournaments
   C.   by exercising daily.
   D.   (no mistakes)

6. A.   Breathing deeply when
   B.   you exercise brings
   C.   Oxygen into your lungs.
   D.   (no mistakes)

7. A.   Muscles and Joints get
   B.   stronger and more
   C.   flexible as you use them.
   D.   (no mistakes)

8. A.   Sarah Hughes was very
   B.   flexible last february;
   C.   she won a gold medal.
   D.   (no mistakes)

Choose your answer carefully. More than one choice may *seem* correct.

Name: _____   Date: _____

Lesson One: Mechanics (cont.)

9. A.   Do you know how many
    B.   Nations belong to the
    C.   United Nations?
    D.   (no mistakes)

10. A.   The United Nations was
    B.   started in 1945, right
    C.   after world war II.
    D.   (no mistakes)

11. A.   When the UN first began,
    B.   it met in San
    C.   Francisco, california.
    D.   (no mistakes)

12. A.   There were 50 nations
    B.   in the beginning; today
    C.   There are 189 countries.
    D.   (no mistakes)

13. A.   UN day, a big event, is
    B.   celebrated every year
    C.   on October 24th.
    D.   (no mistakes)

14. A.   The UN has its own fire
    B.   department, security
    C.   force, and postal service.
    D.   (no mistakes)

15. A.   Ban Ki-moon from
    B.   south Korea is the head
    C.   of the United Nations.
    D.   (no mistakes)

16. A.   He studied at harvard university
    B.   at the Kennedy School
    C.   of Government.
    D.   (no mistakes)

Punctuation

> **Directions:** Look for the mistake in punctuation in each of the sentences in items #17–28.

17. A.   Ants are amazing They
    B.   have survived
    C.   for many years.
    D.   (no mistakes)

18. A.   Scientists estimate that there
    B.   are 20,000 different kinds
    C.   of ants in the world
    D.   (no mistakes)

19. A.   Ants don't have lungs
    B.   They breathe through
    C.   tiny holes in their sides.
    D.   (no mistakes)

Think twice before you change an answer! Your first guess is usually the best guess.

Name: _____ Date: _____

Lesson One: Mechanics (cont.)

20. A.   What do ants eat?
     B.   They like sweets seeds
     C.   and other insects.
     D.   (no mistakes)

21. A.   Did you know that an ant
     B.   can lift 50 times
     C.   its own body weight.
     D.   (no mistakes)

22. A.   Walruses are interesting
     B.   animals too They belong
     C.   to the seal family.
     D.   (no mistakes)

23. A.   They spend most of
     B.   their time in the cold
     C.   water and on ice?
     D.   (no mistakes)

24. A.   The skin of a walrus
     B.   is thick wrinkled and
     C.   almost hairless.
     D.   (no mistakes)

25. A.   They have long sharp
     B.   canine teeth they use
     C.   to scrape up food.
     D.   (no mistakes)

26. A.   They use the teeth to fight
     B.   and even polar bears
     C.   are afraid of them.
     D.   (no mistakes)

27. A.   Komodo dragons bite
     B.   their prey The victim
     C.   then gets sick and dies.
     D.   (no mistakes)

28. A.   This giant lizard then
     B.   returns afterwards
     C.   to eat the body.
     D.   (no mistakes)

If you <u>have</u> to change an answer, **BE SURE** you erase your first answer completely. If the correcting machine sees two circles darkened, it counts both answers wrong.

Name: _____ Date: _____

Lesson One: Mechanics (cont.)

Directions: Look for the mistakes in punctuation in the letter in items #29–35.

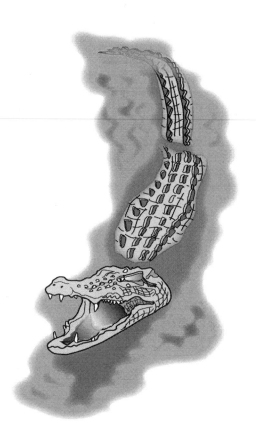

29. A. 416 Hardent Road
    B. Farmington, MI 48240
    C. January, 23 2003
    D. (no mistakes)

30. A. Dear Jeana
    B. Are you looking forward
    C. to our spring vacation?
    D. (no mistakes)

31. A. I have wanted to go to Florida
    B. for a very long time!
    C. I can't wait; can you!
    D. (no mistakes)

32. A. "We are going to the
    B. Everglades" my mom
    C. said at dinner last night.
    D. (no mistakes)

33. A. I know you will like that,
    B. because they have alligators
    C. crocodiles, snakes, and other things.
    D. (no mistakes)

34. A. It won't be long now,
    B. Aren't you excited?
    C. I sure am.
    D. (no mistakes)

35. A. Your best friend
    B. Brianna
    C. (no mistakes)

Name: _____ Date: _____

Lesson One: Mechanics (cont.)

Usage

Standard English is the kind of language you read in books.

Directions: Items #36–45 are testing your use of words. It will show how well you can use words according to the standards of correctly written English. Read the stories, looking for mistakes in how words are used.

36. A. My cousin Savita and I
    B. lived in different places.
    C. Now we is neighbors.
    D. (no mistakes)

37. A. We live in the country
    B. and often see deers in
    C. our backyards.
    D. (no mistakes)

38. A. My cousin was very
    B. impressed when the
    C. leafs changed colors!
    D. (no mistakes)

39. A. Mother and me tried
    B. to explain to her why
    C. they changed colors.
    D. (no mistakes)

40. A. She didn't really get it
    B. but pretended that she did.
    C. Alot of people do that.
    D. (no mistakes)

41. A. Savita gots lots of funny
    B. ideas. She believes a
    C. pixie paints the trees.
    D. (no mistakes)

42. A. She was also surprised
    B. the first time she seed
    C. snow.
    D. (no mistakes)

43. A. My cousin tracked
    B. snow into the house. She
    C. yelled, "Who leaved the door open?"
    D. (no mistakes)

44. A. We had the bestest time.
    B. We played in the snow
    C. until suppertime.
    D. (no mistakes)

45. A. It was fun for days until
    B. all the snow gone away.
    C. It sure was pretty.
    D. (no mistakes)

Name: _____ Date: _____

Lesson One: Mechanics (cont.)

> **Directions:** In questions #46–50, choose the best answer based on the following story.

> ¹This morning, we began our vacation. ²We drove to the airport, parked the car, and got on our airplane. ³<u>My family and me</u> traveled for four hours. ⁴My brother and I played with our Gameboys™. ⁵I don't like Gameboy™. ⁶Both of us fell asleep during the movie. ⁷We woke up just in time to have lunch! ⁸Finally, we landed and got off the plane. ⁹Aunt Carol and Uncle Ken were waiting for us.

46. What is the best way to write sentence 1?
    A. We began our vacation this morning.
    B. Our vacation began this morning.
    C. This morning, we started vacationing.
    D. no change

Avoid making answer sheet errors.

47. Which sentence should be left out of this story?
    A. sentence 3
    B. sentence 5
    C. sentence 7
    D. sentence 9

48. What would be the best way to say the underlined words in sentence 3?
    A. Me and my family
    B. All of my family
    C. My family and I
    D. no change

49. What would be the best way to combine sentences 6 and 7?
    A. Both of us fell asleep during the movie but woke up in time to have lunch.
    B. After falling asleep during the movie, we woke just in time to have lunch.
    C. We fell asleep, and then we woke up.
    D. no change

50. Choose the best last sentence to add to this story.
    A. And we were very happy!
    B. Vacation, here we come!
    C. It finally felt like vacation!
    D. none of these

Name: _____ Date: _____

Lesson One: Mechanics (cont.)

> **Directions:** Choose the correct word to fill in the blank on items #51–55.

51. Amanda _____ about her new puppy all year.
    A.   talk   C.   talking
    B.   talked   D.   have talked

52. The package you have been waiting for _____ yesterday.
    A.   will come   C.   came
    B.   coming   D.   comes

53. Doctors will try to _____ the cure for the disease.
    A.   find   B.   found   C.   have found   D.   has found

54. I _____ to wear my red silky shirt yesterday.
    A.   choose   B.   chose   C.   have chosen D.   chosen

55. Ricky worked _____ on his drawing.
    A.   carefully   B.   careful   C.   carefulness   D.   caring

> **Directions:** Items #56–75 will show how well you can spell. Read each set of words, looking for mistakes in spelling. Circle the letter of the misspelled word. Some sets do not have a mistake.

56. A.   dalight
     B.   sunshine
     C.   nighttime
     D.   no mistake

57. A.   tomorrow
     B.   denim
     C.   fib
     D.   no mistake

58. A.   farmer
     B.   ranebow
     C.   health
     D.   no mistake

59. A.   tomato
     B.   hottest
     C.   roling
     D.   no mistake

60. A.   awful
     B.   baloon
     C.   college
     D.   no mistake

61. A.   radeo
     B.   music
     C.   horse
     D.   no mistake

Make sure that the number you fill in on the answer sheet matches the question number on the test.

Name: _____ Date: _____

Lesson One: Mechanics (cont.)

62. A. ate
    B. eat
    C. eatten
    D. no mistake

63. A. ferry
    B. quiet
    C. beddtime
    D. no mistake

64. A. luving
    B. harm
    C. radios
    D. no mistake

65. A. niece
    B. grammother
    C. aunt
    D. no mistake

66. A. sick
    B. headache
    C. feever
    D. no mistake

67. A. small
    B. pownd
    C. planes
    D. no mistake

68. A. fail
    B. plot
    C. races
    D. no mistake

69. A. closed
    B. library
    C. offise
    D. no mistake

70. A. puppies
    B. caige
    C. fish
    D. no mistake

71. A. teech
    B. happy
    C. bed
    D. no mistake

72. A. art
    B. math
    C. sience
    D. no mistake

Read all of the answers before choosing one.

Name: _____   Date: _____

Lesson One: Mechanics (cont.)

73. A. stay
  B. arriv
  C. home
  D. no mistake

74. A. rite
  B. closet
  C. brave
  D. no mistake

75. A. blanket
  B. towel
  C. qwilt
  D. no mistake

Review

1. Read <u>all</u> directions carefully.

2. Choose your answers carefully. More than one choice may *seem* correct.

3. Think twice before you change an answer.

4. If you **have** to change an answer, be sure you erase your mistake completely.

5. Standard English is the kind of language you read in books or hear on the news.

6. Avoid making answer sheet errors.

7. Make sure the number you fill in on the answer sheet matches the question number on the test.

8. Read <u>all</u> of the answer choices before choosing one.

Name: _____   Date: _____

Unit Two: Language

Lesson Two: Expression

These directions are asking you to choose <u>the best</u>. That means to choose the one in Standard English—the kind of language found in books and in school.

Directions:
Choose the sentence that sounds the best.

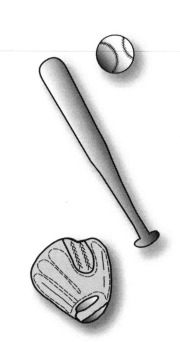

1. A. To the next game, are you going, Jim?
   B. Are you going, Jim, to the next game?
   C. Jim, are you going to the next game?
   D. Going, are you, to the next game?

2. A. Dad and I always go to the game together.
   B. Together to the game, Dad and I always go.
   C. Always to the game together, Dad and I go.
   D. Always to the game, Dad and I go together.

3. A. A home run Kevin hit at the last game.
   B. Kevin hit a home run at the last game.
   C. At the last game, Kevin hit a home run.
   D. Kevin, at the last game, hit a home run.

4. A. First we get hot dogs and sodas at the game.
   B. Hot dogs and sodas at the game first we get.
   C. At the game we get hot dogs and sodas first.
   D. Hot dogs and sodas first we get at the game.

5. A. Finding our seats we sometimes have trouble.
   B. We sometimes have trouble finding our seats.
   C. Sometimes we have trouble finding our seats.
   D. Our seats, sometimes, we have trouble finding.

6. A. As soon as we found our seats, it started to rain.
   B. It started to rain as soon as we found our seats.
   C. Our seats we found as soon as it started to rain.
   D. We found our seats as soon as it started to rain.

Name: _____ Date: _____

Lesson Two: Expression (cont.)

7. A.   The players slipped running to the dugout.
    B.   To the dugout, the players slipped running.
    C.   Running to the dugout, the players slipped.
    D.   Slipped the players to the dugout running.

> Stay calm … focus on the task at hand.

8. A.   At last the sun came out, and so did the ballplayers.
    B.   The ballplayers and the sun both came out at last.
    C.   The sun came out and at last so did the ballplayers.
    D.   Out came the ballplayers and so did the sun.

9. A.   Bonds hit a home run while eating my pizza.
    B.   While eating my pizza, Bonds hit a home run.
    C.   Bonds, while eating my pizza, hit a home run.
    D.   While I was eating my pizza, Bonds hit a home run.

10. A.   To win the game, the players must hit many home runs.
    B.   Many home runs must the players hit to win the game.
    C.   Many home runs must be hit by the players to win the game.
    D.   Home runs must be hit by many players to win the game.

Directions:

For items #11–15, choose the word that correctly completes each sentence.

> Clear your mind of everything but this test!

11. Melissa and _____ went to the theater on Sunday.
    A.   her
    B.   she
    C.   him
    D.   them

12. Laura invited Tana and _____ to her dance recital.
    A.   they
    B.   me
    C.   we
    D.   I

Name: _____   Date: _____

Lesson Two: Expression (cont.)

13. Why is Karla so careful when _____ bakes bread?
    A. he
    B. she
    C. I
    D. they

14. They ate dinner with _____ last night.
    A. us
    B. we
    C. she
    D. they

> Don't spend too much time on any one question.

15. _____ played soccer on the same team.
    A. Them
    B. They
    C. Him
    D. Their

Directions:
For items #16–20, choose the word that can be used in place of the under-lined word or words.

---

16. Everyone in the class was happy for <u>Tommy</u>.
    A. me   B. her   C. him   D. them

17. Blair put <u>the puppies</u> near the warm heater.
    A. them   B. their   C. it   D. him

18. <u>Shelly and Sherwood</u> built their own playhouse.
    A. Them   B. Their   C. They   D. Your

19. The fourth grade gave a big party for <u>Delia</u>.
    A. she   B. he   C. him   D. her

20. Bob, when did you lose <u>your mittens</u>?
    A. they   B. their   C. them   D. it

Name: _____ Date: _____

Lesson Two: Expression (cont.)

Directions:
For items #21–25, choose the underlined word or words that is/are the simple subject of each sentence.

---

21. <u>Eleven</u> <u>girls</u> practiced <u>cheerleading</u> after <u>school</u>.
    A   B   C   D

> Do the easy ones first. Then if you have time, go back and try the harder ones.

22. <u>Our</u> new <u>television</u> has a <u>flat</u> <u>screen</u>.
    A   B   C   D

23. The <u>race</u> will <u>start</u> in the <u>park</u> after <u>dark</u>.
        A   B   C   D

24. <u>Ruth</u> won the <u>spelling bee</u> <u>contest</u> in the <u>third</u> grade.
    A   B   C   D

25. <u>We</u> baked <u>cupcakes</u> for my <u>birthday</u> party <u>yesterday</u>.
    A   B   C   D

Directions:
For items #26–30, choose the underlined word or words that is/are the simple predicate of each sentence.

---

26. <u>My</u> dad <u>cooked</u> the <u>hot dogs</u> on <u>the</u> grill last night.
    A   B   C   D

27. Ramon <u>ran</u> all the <u>way</u> to the <u>bus</u> <u>stop</u>.
        A   B   C   D

> Check to **BE SURE** the test question numbers match the answer sheet numbers.

28. Elton <u>knew</u> the <u>way</u> to the <u>village</u> <u>green</u>.
        A   B   C   D

29. <u>Mrs. Glue</u> and <u>Mr. Glubber</u> <u>telephoned</u> the <u>school</u>.
        A   B   C   D

30. <u>My</u> father and my <u>mother</u> <u>read</u> <u>magazines</u>.
    A   B   C   D

Name: _____   Date: _____

Lesson Two: Expression (cont.)

Directions:
For items #31–35, read each pair of sentences. Then choose the sentence that best combines the two sentences.

---

31. Our class is going to the zoo.
    We are going on Friday.

    A. To the zoo our class is going on Friday.
    B. Our class on Friday is going to the zoo.
    C. Friday to the zoo our class is going.
    D. On Friday, our class is going to the zoo.

Take all of the time allowed. If you finish early, reread the questions and your answers.

32. Holly said farewell to her old neighbors.
    She said hello to her new neighbors.

    A. After saying farewell to her old neighbors, Holly said hello to her new neighbors.
    B. Holly said hello to her new neighbors after she said farewell to her old neighbors.
    C. Holly said farewell to her old neighbors and then said hello to her new neighbors.
    D. After saying hello to her new neighbors, Holly said farewell to her old neighbors.

33. Katie forgot her lunch today.
    Her mother brought it to her.

    A. Katie's mother brought her lunch because she forgot it.
    B. Today, Katie forgot her lunch, and her mother brought it to her.
    C. Because she forgot her lunch, Katie's mother brought it.
    D. Katie forgot her lunch today, but her mother brought it to her.

34. My kitten was hiding.
    She was hiding under the bed.

    A. My kitten was hiding under the bed.
    B. Under the bed, my kitten was hiding.
    C. Hiding under the bed was my kitten.
    D. Hiding my kitten was under the bed.

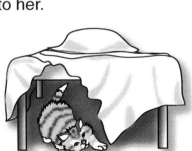

Name: _____ Date: _____

Lesson Two: Expression (cont.)

35. My brother chopped wood.
    My brother stacked wood.

    A.   My brother chopped and stacked wood.
    B.   The wood was chopped and stacked by my brother.
    C.   Chopped the wood and stacked the wood my brother did.
    D.   The wood was chopped and stacked by my brother.

Directions:
Read the story below, and then answer questions #36–40.

---

[1]The first human being to travel in space was a Soviet cosmonaut. [2]Yuri Gagarin. [3]He shot into space on the *Vostok 1* on April 12, 1961. [4]He circled the earth in 108 minutes. [5]Earth is part of the Milky Way galaxy. [6]He landed by parachute only six miles from his planned landing spot. [7]He remained a cosmonaut until he died in a plane crash in 1968.

36. Which group of words in the story above is not a sentence?
    A.   2
    B.   4
    C.   6
    D.   All of them are sentences

37. Which sentence does not belong in the story?
    A.   1
    B.   3
    C.   5
    D.   7

A paragraph focuses on <u>one</u> main idea.

38. Which sentence tells the main idea of the report?
    A.   1
    B.   2
    C.   5
    D.   6

Name: _____ Date: _____

Lesson Two: Expression (cont.)

39. What is the best way to combine sentences 4 and 6?
    A. In 108 minutes, he circled the earth and landed by parachute.
    B. He circled the earth in 108 minutes and landed by parachute.
    C. After circling the earth in 108 minutes, he landed by parachute only six miles from his planned landing spot.
    D. Six miles from his planned landing spot, he landed by parachute after circling the earth in 108 minutes.

40. What is the best way to conclude this report?
    A. He died in a plane crash in 1968.
    B. Still a cosmonaut in 1968, Yuri Gagarin died in a plane crash.
    C. Sadly, Gagarin died in a plane crash in 1968.
    D. Leave it as it is.

> ### Directions:
> For items #41–45, read each sentence. Then choose the sentence that does __not__ provide supporting details for that sentence.

41. Mrs. Gurney is our grouchy neighbor next door.
    A. She yells at me if I walk on her grass.
    B. She yells at me if my ball goes in her backyard.
    C. She yells at me if my dog barks too much.
    D. My dog is black and white.

42. The night the lights went out, we were robbed.
    A. We went to the movies that night.
    B. The movie was a very good one.
    C. When we got home, we noticed the lights were all off.
    D. Dad's flashlight showed us what the robbers took.

Say the answer choices softly to yourself. Choose the best one—the one that sounds like your teacher might use it.

43. Janelle's family owns a restaurant.
    A. Everyone in the family works at the restaurant.
    B. Janelle buses the tables.
    C. Antonio washes the dishes.
    D. Her mother is very pretty.

Name: _____ Date: _____

Lesson Two: Expression (cont.)

44. Kolby and his family are moving.
    A.   Kolby is my best friend.
    B.   When he moves, I will really miss him.
    C.   People ski in Colorado.
    D.   He's going to Colorado with his family.

45. My Granny and Poppa live on a farm.
    A.   They are my dad's parents.
    B.   Granny keeps chickens and pigs.
    C.   The farm is far away.
    D.   Poppa takes care of the cows and crops.

Directions:
For items #46–50, read each story. Choose the best ending for each story.

---

46. DeWayne and Aisha built a fort in their backyard. Their mother helped them. De-Wayne found directions in one of the magazines he got from the library.

    A.   The End
    B.   It was hard work, but they really enjoyed it.
    C.   They were happy when it was done.
    D.   When they finished the fort, they celebrated.

47. The Lees have a cat named Felix. Felix is big, black, and mean. He either sleeps in the sun all day or chases after mice. Sometimes he bites the Lees' guests.

    A.   Even the Lees don't like Felix very much.
    B.   Everyone hates Felix.
    C.   Felix is dangerous.
    D.   Who likes Felix?

Eliminate obviously wrong choices. Take your best guess from those remaining.

48. Be careful when you go out this morning. It rained, and the cold made the rain freeze. The sidewalks and roads are very slippery.

    A.   People could get hurt.   C.   You could go ice skating.
    B.   I hate winter.   D.   We wanted it to snow.

Name: _____   Date: _____

Lesson Two: Expression (cont.)

49. Every Thanksgiving, the Menard family goes to Aunt Barb's for dinner. There are aunts, uncles, cousins, nieces, nephews, and a few strangers hanging around the kitchen. There are so many people that sometimes there isn't anywhere to sit.

   A.   Aunt Barb serves turkey and gravy.
   B.   Aunt Jo makes the pies.
   C.   Thanksgiving for the Menards is a family affair.
   D.   I like Uncle Steve's bread.

50. Crack! Thomas hit the ball so far and so hard he broke the neighbor's window. Thomas tried to tell the neighbor lady it was his fault, but she wasn't home. He wanted to be there when the lady came home and saw the broken window.

   A.   He felt responsible for the damage.
   B.   He wanted to tell her it wasn't his fault.
   C.   The lady would be so surprised.
   D.   Thomas had a really bad day.

Review

1. Remember, *Standard English* is the language in books and used in school.
2. Stay calm … focus on the test.
3. Clear your mind of everything but this test.
4. Don't spend too much time on any one item.
5. Do the easy ones first, and then if there is time, go back and try the harder ones.
6. Check to be sure the test question numbers match the answer sheet numbers.
7. Take all the time allowed. Reread the questions and your answers if you finish early.
8. Remember, a paragraph focuses on only one main idea.
9. Say the answer choices softly to yourself when determining what sounds best.
10. Use the process of elimination to get rid of obviously wrong choices.

Name: _____　Date: _____

UNIT TWO: LANGUAGE

Lesson Three: Information Skills

Directions:
This is a test about using reference materials. Four answers are given for each question. Choose the answer you think is better than the others.

---

1. Which question could you answer using a dictionary?
   A.　How much does a *cobbler* charge?
   B.　What is a *cobbler*?
   C.　What materials does a *cobbler* use?
   D.　What is the best way to train as a *cobbler*?

"Better than the others," may mean that more than one answer may be right. Choose the best one.

2. Which would you find in a dictionary?
   A.　The history of baseball
   B.　The meaning of the word *baseball*
   C.　A story about baseball
   D.　The rules for playing baseball

3. For which purpose would you first use an encyclopedia?
   A.　To find out about the country of Guyana
   B.　To find a story about the people of Guyana
   C.　To find out how to get to Guyana
   D.　To find out about other countries around Guyana

4. Where would you look to find out about what the weather in the Philippine Islands will be in October?
   A.　A dictionary
   B.　An atlas
   C.　A biography
   D.　A storybook

Budget your time wisely.

5. Where would you look to find the most information about hiking?
   A.　In a newspaper
   B.　In an encyclopedia
   C.　In a dictionary
   D.　In a geography book

Name: _____ Date: _____

Lesson Three: Information Skills (cont.)

Tricky one! Both A and C could be right, but C is the better answer. Why?

6. Where would you look to find out how to spell hippopotamus?
   A. In a spelling book
   B. In an encyclopedia
   C. In a dictionary
   D. In a history book

7. Which section of a library would have a book about starting a coin collection?
   A. Fiction
   B. Nonfiction
   C. Biography
   D. Reference

8. Below are the results of an electronic search using *holidays* as a key word. Which one would tell about St. Patrick's Day?
   A. Holiday Listing and Descriptions
   B. Holiday Greeting Cards
   C. Holiday Crafts and Pictures
   D. Daily Holidays

9. Which of these Web pages would be useful for finding information about the solar system?
   A. Africam
   B. Bonus.com
   C. DISNEY for Kids
   D. National Geographic for Kids

10. Which of the following kids' news resources is written incorrectly?
   A. www.msnbc.com/local/pencilnews/
   B. www.weeklyreader.com/features/kids.html
   C. www.abcnews.go.com/abcnews4kids/kids
   D. www.kidsnewsroom

Name: _____   Date: _____

Lesson Three: Information Skills (cont.)

Directions:
Use this page from the dictionary and the pronunciation guide below it to answer questions #11–18.

Ff

footlights *plural noun* Lights placed in a row along the front of a stage floor in a theater.
foot•lights (fŏot′ līts′) ◊ *plural noun*

footman *noun* A male servant who opens doors and waits on tables.
foot•man (fŏot′ mən) ◊ *noun, plural* **footmen**

footnote *noun* A note at the bottom of a page that explains something in the text.
foot•note (fŏot′ nōt′) ◊ *noun, plural* **footnotes**

footprint *noun* A mark left by a foot.
foot•print (fŏot′ print′) ◊ *noun, plural* **footprints**

footsore *adjective* Having sore or tired feet from much walking: *footsore hikers.*
foot•sore (fŏot′ sôr′) ◊ *adjective*

footstep *noun* 1. A step of the foot. 2. The sound of a step. 3. A footprint.
foot•step (fŏot′ stĕp′) ◊ *noun, plural* **footsteps**

footstool *noun* A low stool on which to rest the feet while sitting.
foot•stool (fŏot′ stōol′) ◊ *noun, plural* **footstools**

footwear *noun* Coverings for the feet, such as shoes and boots.
foot•wear (fŏot′ wâr′) ◊ *noun*

for *preposition* 1. Directed or sent to: *There's a package for you on the table.* 2. As a result of: *She cheered for joy.* 3. Through the duration of: *He worked for an hour.* 4. In order to go to or reach: *We started for home early in the morning.* 5. With the purpose of finding, getting, having, keeping, or saving: *I was looking for a bargain.*
for (fôr) ◊ *preposition*

ă	pat	ĭ	pit	oi	oil	th	bath
ā	pay	ī	ride	ŏŏ	book	th	bathe
â	care	î	fierce	ōŏ	boot	ə	ago, item
ä	father	ŏ	pot	ou	out		pencil
ĕ	pet	ō	go	ŭ	cut		atom
ē	be	ô	paw, for	û	fur		circus

11. Upon which item would you rest your feet while watching TV?
    A. footnote
    B. footsore
    C. footstool
    D. footwear

12. The **ea** in *footwear* sounds like the *a* in
    A. father
    B. pay
    C. pat
    D. care

13. What is another word for shoes and boots?
    A. footwear
    B. footstep
    C. footprint
    D. footman

14. How do you spell the word for a man-servant who opens doors?
    A. footsore
    B. footstep
    C. footman
    D. footnote

15. Which word fits best in the sentence, "The hikers were _____ after their 5-mile hike."?
    A. footlight
    B. footprints
    C. footsore
    D. footnote

Name: _____   Date: _____

Lesson Three: Information Skills (cont.)

16. Which word best fits the sentence, "We went shopping _____ great bargains."?
    A. for
    B. footsteps
    C. footstool
    D. footnote

17. Which word best fits the sentence, "She walked along the shore, leaving her _____ in the sand."?
    A. footlights
    B. footwear
    C. footprints
    D. footsteps

Why is C a better answer than D?

18. Which word best fits the sentence, "Did you include _____ in your report?"?
    A. footwear
    B. footnotes
    C. footlights
    D. footsteps

Directions:
For items #19–24, choose the word or name that would come first in a dictionary or encyclopedia.

---

19. A. Hungary
    B. hunting
    C. hummingbird
    D. human being

20. A. cheese
    B. Chile
    C. chess
    D. chemistry

21. A. dream
    B. duck
    C. drum
    D. donkey

22. A. Gutenberg, Johann
    B. Gulf War
    C. guitar
    D. guinea pig

23. A. Ecuador
    B. Ethiopia
    C. England
    D. Europe

24. A. Northern Ireland
    B. Nobel Prize
    C. North Pole
    D. nomad

Name: _____ Date: _____

Lesson Three: Information Skills (cont.)

25. Which of these words would you find on a dictionary page with the guide words *knee* and *knot*?
    A. known
    B. knob
    C. know
    D. koala

26. Which of these words would you find on a dictionary page with the guide words *pointer* and *pole*?
    A. polish
    B. police
    C. polecat
    D. poison ivy

Use the process of elimination to find the answer.

Think twice before changing an answer.

Directions:
Use this table of contents to answer questions #27–31.

Table of Contents

Chapter	Contents	Page
1	Animal News and Facts	3
2	Animal Babies	10
3	Animal Habitats	21
4	Endangered Species	32
5	Pets	40
6	The World of Dinosaurs	56

27. Which of these would Chapter 3 tell you the most about?
    A. How animals become endangered
    B. What groups of animals are called
    C. Where animals live
    D. Where animals migrate

Name: _____ Date: _____

Lesson Three: Information Skills (cont.)

28. Which chapter could tell you the name of the biggest venomous snake?
    A.   Chapter 1
    B.   Chapter 3
    C.   Chapter 4
    D.   Chapter 6

29. Where should you look to find out about kits, cubs, hatchlings, and joeys?
    A.   Page 10
    B.   Page 40
    C.   Page 21
    D.   Page 3

30. If you wanted to find out the names of the ten most popular dogs, where would you look?
    A.   Chapter 3
    B.   Chapter 4
    C.   Chapter 5
    D.   Chapter 6

31. Which would Chapter 6 tell you most about?
    A.   How to classify different animals
    B.   How to find the world's oldest fossilized vomit
    C.   How to learn more about worms
    D.   The ten most popular pet names

Directions:
For items #32–36, read the questions about computers. Then choose the correct answer.

Use logical reasoning to choose the best answer.

32. Which of the following do you use to move the cursor on the screen and click?
    A.   the disk
    B.   the screen
    C.   the mouse
    D.   the keyboard

Name: _____ Date: _____

Lesson Three: Information Skills (cont.)

33. Which of the following do you use to type on the computer screen?
    A. the disk
    B. the screen
    C. the mouse
    D. the keyboard

34. Which of the following do you use to store your work?
    A. the disk
    B. the screen
    C. the mouse
    D. the keyboard

35. When you want to store your work on a disk or on the computer, what command do you give?
    A. open
    B. save
    C. exit
    D. paste

36. When you want to end what you are doing on the computer, what command do you give?
    A. stop
    B. save
    C. exit
    D. edit

Directions:
Use this page from a telephone book to answer questions #37–40.

BOBLITT Russel W 101 Maple Ln Rochstr . 555-9076
BOCH D L & John 3306 Stanton.................. 555-8144
   John 134 8th St Lincoln......................... 555-4027
   Karrie 101 Oscar St Lincoln 555-5407
   Robt E 325 Northgate St 555-3269
BOCHENEK Stephen J atty 607 E Adams .. 555-1144
   Stephen J 2249 Warson Rd 555-1293
BOCK Adam 2202 N Kickapoo St Lincoln 555-1551
   Adam F 215 Crestwood Dr Lincoln......... 555-6536
   Amy & Steven 710 Trojan Rd Auburn 555-4126
   B 3361 Spring S View 555-3893
   Daniel W 320 Northgate 555-4337
   Geo L 1056 Green Acres Ln................... 555-7438
   Lawrence L 69 Red Fox Ct 555-6381
   Roger 450 450th Av Wlmsvl 555-3867
   Roger & Loretta 18 Bitterroot Dr Athns . 555-8619
   Wayne Elkhart 555-2228

37. How many entries for the name Bock are in this phone book?
    A. 1
    B. 5
    C. 7
    D. 10

38. How many of the residents on this page live in Lincoln?
    A. 2
    B. 4
    C. 5
    D. 8

Name: _____ Date: _____

Lesson Three: Information Skills (cont.)

39. What is Stephen J. Bochenek's job?
    A. He is a doctor.
    B. He is a dentist.
    C. He is an attorney.
    D. He is a veterinarian.

40. What number would you call to reach Karrie Boch?
    A. 555-5407
    B. 555-9076
    C. 555-1293
    D. 555-4027

Review

1. Budget your time wisely.
2. "Better than the others" means more than one answer may be right. Choose the <u>best</u> one.
3. Use the process of elimination to find the answer.
4. Think twice before changing an answer.
5. Use logical reasoning (e.g., What makes the best sense?).

Helpful Math Strategies

Test Tips

1. Use all of the time that is provided. This is a test, not a race.
2. Use your time wisely.
3. Do not spend too much time on any one answer.
4. Skip hard questions and do the easy ones first. Then go back and do the hard ones.
5. Read each question carefully. Read it twice if you need to.
6. Think twice before you change an answer.

Math Strategies

★ Look at the signs carefully in the problem. Know if you are being asked to add, subtract, multiply, or divide.

★ Be sure to check your work; the right answer may not be given.

★ Check your work by reversing the problem.

★ Do all of your work on scratch paper.

★ Be sure to transfer the right answer to the answer sheet.

★ Decide if your answers make sense.

★ Study the words in word problems carefully to decide what you have to do to find the answer.

Name: _____　Date: _____

UNIT THREE: MATHEMATICS

Lesson One: Concepts

Use all of the time that is provided. This is a test, not a race.

Directions:
Choose the correct answer for each question.
You will need a metric ruler for some questions.

---

1. How many of the numbers below are smaller than 267?

763	296	259	235

   A.　4
   B.　2
   C.　1
   D.　3

2. Use the table to determine whose class collected the most labels.

Skip hard questions and do the easy ones first. Then go back and do the hard ones.

Class	Labels collected
Mrs. Greene	107
Mr. Browne	98
Ms. Grey	128
Miss White	150

   A.　Mrs. Greene
   B.　Mr. Browne
   C.　Ms. Grey
   D.　Miss White

3. What fraction of the balls are shaded?

  A. $\frac{1}{5}$　　　B. $\frac{2}{5}$　　　C. $\frac{3}{5}$　　　D. $\frac{1}{2}$

Name: _____ Date: _____

Lesson One: Concepts (cont.)

4. What should replace the ☐ in this number sentence?

   24 ☐ 4 = 20

   A. +
   B. −
   C. x
   D. ÷

5. Which number is a multiple of 3?

   A. 31   B. 27   C. 10   D. 2

6. How many square units are in the shaded figure?

   ☐ = 1 square unit

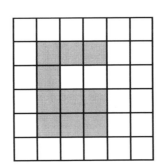

   A. 8
   B. 9
   C. 10
   D. 12

7. Which number is a multiple of 6?

   A. 27   B. 24   C. 45   D. 15

8. Use the centimeter side of your ruler to measure the flagpole from top to bottom.

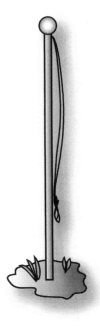

   A. 4 centimeters
   B. 6 centimeters
   C. 7 centimeters
   D. 9 centimeters

Name: _____ Date: _____

Lesson One: Concepts (cont.)

9. What is the best unit for measuring the length of your desk?

   A. inch   B. yard   C. pound   D. ounce

10. The temperature is 85 degrees. Which thermometer shows 85°F?

    A.    B.    C.    D.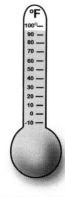

11. Which tool should Tawana use to measure the weight of her apple?

    A. ruler
    B. thermometer
    C. measuring cup
    D. scale

    Read each question carefully. Read it twice if you need to.

12. These oranges weigh 7 ounces each. How much do they weigh all together?

    A. 36 ounces
    B. 42 ounces
    C. 54 ounces
    D. 49 ounces

    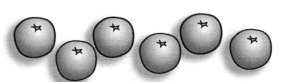

13. Look at the subtraction fact in the box. Then choose the addition fact that belongs to the same fact family.

    A. $9 + 5 = 14$
    B. $6 + 9 = 15$
    C. $6 + 5 = 11$
    D. $8 + 6 = 14$

    $$15 - 9 = 6$$

Name: _____   Date: _____

Lesson One: Concepts (cont.)

14. Which of these shows the number 634?

    A. four hundred thirty-six
    B. six hundred thirty-four
    C. three hundred forty-six
    D. six hundred forty-three

Think twice before you change an answer.

15. Mom made 24 cookies. John ate 11 cookies, and Mary ate 10 cookies. How many cookies were left?

    A. 4
    B. 22
    C. 5
    D. 3

16. Conrad had 25 trading cards. The box in the number sentence is equal to the number of cards his grandmother gave him. How many trading cards did Conrad's grandmother give him?

$$25 + \boxed{} = 37$$

    A. 12   B. 25   C. 37   D. 62

17. Ronald was hired to walk Mrs. Meyer's dogs. He used a number pattern to decide how long to walk the dogs on each day. How long did he walk them on day 6?

Day	1	2	3	4	5	6
Min.	5	10	20	40	80	?

    A. 160   B. 90   C. 150   D. 85

18. Choose the one that would come next in this pattern.

    A.   B.   C.   D.

Name: _____ Date: _____

Lesson One: Concepts (cont.)

19. What should replace the ☐ in the number sentence below?

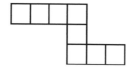

6 + 3 + 2 = 2 + 3 + ☐

     A.   2   B.   6   C.   3   D.   11

20. Look at this shape:

Which of these shows the same shape turned a different way?

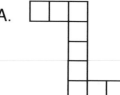 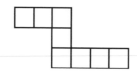 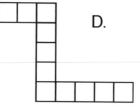 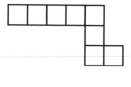

A.   B.   C.   D.

21. Which dotted line is a line of symmetry?

A.   B.   C.   D.

22. Which object in this picture is shaped like a cylinder?

     A.   balloon
     B.   baby's legs
     C.   baby's hat
     D.   blocks

23. Find the perimeter for this object.

     A.   4 ft.
     B.   10 ft.
     C.   6 ft.
     D.   12 ft.

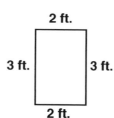

2 ft.   3 ft.   3 ft.   2 ft.

Name: _____ Date: _____

Lesson One: Concepts (cont.)

24. Which of the figures below could be formed by folding Figure 1 along the dotted lines?

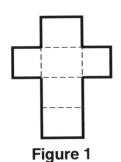  

Figure 1

25. Which of these figures is an open figure with a star inside?

A.   B.   C.   D.

26. Which one of these shows 56 rounded to the nearest 10?
    A. 57   B. 55   C. 60   D. 50

27. What is another way to write 216?
    A. 21 + 6
    B. 20 + 1 + 6
    C. 200 + 100 + 6
    D. 200 + 10 + 6

28. A monkey paused exactly halfway up the ladder. There were 5 rungs behind him. How many rungs were ahead of him?
    A. 1   B. 2   C. 5   D. 10

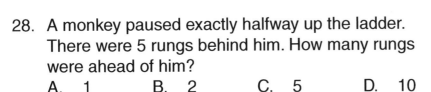

Do not spend too much time on any one question.

29. Which is a list of odd numbers?
    A. 1, 3, 5, 7, 9
    B. 2, 4, 6, 8, 10
    C. 3, 11, 42, 81
    D. 7, 14, 21, 35

Name: _____ Date: _____

Lesson One: Concepts (cont.)

30. What number should replace the ☐ in the number sentence?

    $4 \times \square = 28$

    A. 4   B. 21   C. 7   D. 35

31. In the school raffle, 500 tickets were sold. Raphael bought one ticket. Which of these tells how likely it is that Raphael has the winning ticket?

    A. certain
    B. very likely
    C. unlikely
    D. impossible

32. If you spun this spinner 100 times, which number would the arrow land on the most?

    A. 1
    B. 2
    C. 3
    D. not given

33. Doug is using a spinner. Which color will he be least likely to spin?

    A. blue
    B. green
    C. yellow
    D. red

34. What time is shown on this clock?

    A. 5:00
    B. 12:35
    C. 7:12
    D. 7:00

35. Nick started to play a video game at 1:00. Two and one-half hours later he stopped playing. Which clock shows what time Nick stopped playing the video game?

    A.   B.   C.   D.

Name: _____ Date: _____

Lesson One: Concepts (cont.)

36. The time now is 8:30. What time will it be four and one-half hours from now?

A.    B.    C.    D.

37. Which is the Roman numeral for 59?

    A.   XXXXXVIIII
    B.   LIX
    C.   LVIIII
    D.   CLIX

38. Leah will have her birthday party on the third Wednesday of August. What is the date of Leah's party?

    A.   15
    B.   22
    C.   16
    D.   29

AUGUST						
Sun.	Mon.	Tues.	Wed.	Thurs.	Fri.	Sat.
		1	2	3	4	5
6	7	8	9	10	11	12
13	14	15	16	17	18	19
20	21	22	23	24	25	26
27	28	29	30	31		

39. Uncle Steve's birthday is the 22nd of August. What day of the week will that be?

    A.   Tuesday
    B.   Monday
    C.   Wednesday
    D.   Friday

40. Look at the clock. What time will it be in 40 minutes?

    A.   6:40
    B.   7:00
    C.   7:20
    D.   7:40

Name: _____   Date: _____

Lesson One: Concepts (cont.)

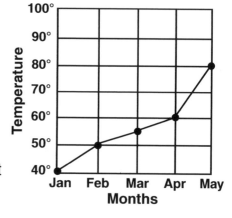

41. Between which two months has there been the greatest change in temperature?

   A.   January - February
   B.   February - March
   C.   March - April
   D.   April - May

42. Using the temperature graph, what is the greatest degree of change between the two months in the question above?

   A.   20°
   B.   15°
   C.   10°
   D.   5°

43. If July 4th is on a Tuesday, what day of the week will July 12th be?

   A.   Tuesday
   B.   Wednesday
   C.   Monday
   D.   not given

Try using all answer choices back in the problem. Which one fits?

44. How much money is this?

   A. $0.76
   B. $0.61
   C. $0.31
   D. $26.00

45. What is the answer to this problem?

   A.   5 dimes
   B.   three dimes, one nickel, two pennies
   C.   four dimes, seven pennies
   D.   5 nickels, 1 dime, 3 pennies

Name: _____   Date: _____

Lesson Two: Computation (cont.)

23. 48 ÷ 6 =

A. 6
B. 8
C. 2
D. not given

24.   632
     x   4

A. 2,528
B. 1,076
C. 2,428
D. not given

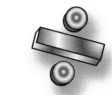

25.   72
     - 12

A. 84
B. 50
C. 60
D. not given

26. Which of the number sentences below is true?

A. 399 < 390
B. 399 > 490
C. 390 = 490
D. 490 > 399

If you work on scratch paper, be sure that you transfer your numbers correctly.

27. $\frac{8}{9}$ - $\frac{4}{9}$ =

A. $\frac{5}{18}$
B. $\frac{4}{9}$
C. $\frac{5}{9}$
D. not given

28. 2,515 ÷ 5 =

A. 503
B. 623
C. 502
D. not given

29. 41 x 500 =

A. 900
B. 2,000
C. 300
D. not given

Name: _____ Date: _____

Lesson Two: Computation (cont.)

30. $\frac{1}{3} + \frac{1}{3} =$

    A. $\frac{1}{9}$

    B. $\frac{1}{3}$

    C. $\frac{2}{3}$

    D. not given

31. $8\overline{)16}$

    A. 4
    B. 12
    C. 2
    D. not given

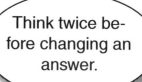

Think twice before changing an answer.

32.   246
    - 86

    A. 160
    B. 320
    C. 332
    D. not given

33. $4.02
    + $2.68

    A. $3.05
    B. $6.70
    C. $7.60
    D. not given

34. $76.40 - $53.80 =

    A. $26.22   C. $22.60
    B. $22.06   D. not given

35.   124
    62
    + 477

    A. 549   C. 663
    B. 562   D. not given

Review

1. Look at the signs carefully to know if you should add, subtract, multiply, or divide.
2. Be sure to check your computations.
3. When you are not sure of an answer, take your best guess.
4. If you work on scratch paper, be sure to transfer the numbers correctly.
5. Think twice before changing an answer.

Name: _____ Date: _____

Lesson Three: Problem Solving and Reasoning (cont.)

11. The Altman farm has 20 large animals. Two-fifths of the animals are horses, two-fifths are cows, and the rest are pigs. What fraction of the animals are pigs?

   A. $\frac{1}{2}$ B. $\frac{1}{4}$ C. $\frac{1}{3}$ D. $\frac{1}{5}$

12. How many horses and cows are on the Altman farm?

   A. 8   B. 6   C. 16   D. 4

13. How many pigs are on the Altman farm?

   A. 8   B. 6   C. 16   D. 4

> **Directions:**
> Use the table of distances between certain cities in the United States to answer questions #14–18.

> Read each answer choice carefully before making your decision.

	Atlanta	Chicago	Dallas	El Paso	Little Rock	Los Angeles	New Orleans	Phila-delphia
Atlanta	X	715	839	1476	362	2289	523	797
Chicago	715	X	971	1483	660	2128	957	757
Dallas	839	971	X	630	343	1450	504	1544
El Paso	1476	1483	630	X	880	810	1124	2132
Little Rock	362	660	343	880	X	1710	438	1200
Los Angeles	2289	2128	1450	810	1710	X	1937	2874
New Orleans	523	957	504	1124	438	1937	X	1276
Philadelphia	797	757	1544	2132	1200	2874	1276	X

14. How many miles is it from Los Angeles to El Paso?

   A. 810   B. 880   C. 630   D. 438

15. How many miles is it from Los Angeles to Philadelphia?

   A. 2,289   B. 1,937   C. 2,132   D. 2,874

16. Which city is farthest from Little Rock?

   A. Chicago   B. Los Angeles   C. Philadelphia   D. El Paso

Name: _____ Date: _____

Lesson Three: Problem Solving and Reasoning (cont.)

17. How much farther is it from Dallas to Atlanta than from Los Angeles to El Paso?

    A. 20 mi.   B. 25 mi.   C. 29 mi.   D. 50 mi.

18. The Casey family is traveling from their home in New Orleans to visit family in Los Angeles. They want to go the shortest route with only one stopover. Which city would make the best stopover?

    A. Dallas   B. El Paso   C. Little Rock   D. Chicago

19. Which of these combinations of coins does not equal 55 cents?
    A. 2 quarters, 1 nickel
    B. 5 dimes, 1 nickel
    C. 1 quarter, 2 nickels, 2 dimes
    D. 4 dimes, 2 nickels

20. What is the next number in this pattern?

    70, 65, 60, 55, _____

    A. 75   B. 45   C. 50   D. 80

21. The doctor measured the height of the three Baker children. Whitney was 51 inches tall, Hugh was 48 inches tall, and Spencer was $52\frac{1}{2}$ inches tall. How much taller is Spencer than Hugh?

    A. 3 inches   B. $4\frac{1}{2}$ inches   C. $1\frac{1}{2}$ inches   D. not given

22. Bernita ran 320 yards from school to her house. Then she ran 290 yards to Yolanda's house. Together, the two girls ran 545 yards to the mall. How many yards in all did Bernita run?

    A. 1,155 yards
    B. 865 yards
    C. 610 yards
    D. not given

Decide if your answers make sense.

Name: _____ Date: _____

Lesson Three: Problem Solving and Reasoning (cont.)

23. Which fraction tells you what part of the figure is shaded?

A. $\frac{5}{6}$ C. $\frac{5}{9}$

B. $\frac{4}{5}$ D. $\frac{9}{5}$

24. Which figure is equivalent to the fraction $\frac{2}{3}$?

A.   B.   C.   D.

25. Which fraction is bigger than $\frac{1}{4}$?

A. $\frac{1}{6}$ C. $\frac{4}{8}$

B. $\frac{2}{8}$ D. $\frac{1}{8}$

26. Which is the correct way to write 700 + 60 + 5 ?

A.   7,650
B.   765
C.   7,506
D.   not given

27. Which set of coins is worth the most money?

A.   15 pennies
B.   2 quarters
C.   4 dimes
D.   8 nickels

Try each answer choice in the problem. Which one makes the most sense?

Name: _____   Date: _____

Lesson Three: Problem Solving and Reasoning (cont.)

28. Which of the following would you use to estimate the cost of a large popcorn at $2.39 and a large soda at $1.75 at the movie theater?

    A. $2.40 + $1.80
    B. $5.50 + $2.00
    C. $2.00 + $1.00
    D. $3.00 + $2.00

29. Which is the closest estimate of $678 - $310?

    A. $700 - $300   C. $600 - $400
    B. $600 - $300   D. $700 - $400

30. What number should come next in this counting pattern?

523	528	533	538

    A.   543   C.   548
    B.   542   D.   553

Review

1. Study the words in each problem carefully to decide what you need to do to find the answer.

2. Look for words or numbers in the question that tell you what information to find.

3. Read each answer choice carefully before making your decision.

4. Decide if your answers make sense.

5. Try each answer choice in the problem. Which one makes the most sense?

Helpful Science Strategies

Test Tips

1. Skip the hard questions, and answer the easy ones first.
2. Think twice before changing an answer.
3. Answer all questions.
4. When all else fails, guess.
5. Avoid making answer sheet errors.

Science Strategies

★ Pay close attention to how each question is worded. All answers may be *true*, but only one answers the question.

★ Use logical reasoning to answer the question. Does your answer make sense?

★ Use the process of elimination to find answers. Cross out those choices that you *know* are wrong.

★ Examine charts, pictures, diagrams, and figures carefully. They will provide you with extra information.

Name: _____ Date: _____

UNIT FOUR: SCIENCE

Lesson One: Process and Inquiry

Directions:
Choose the best answer for each question.

1. Scientists use scientific methods to
   A. find answers to their questions.
   B. find questions for their answers.
   C. solve the many problems they have.
   D. prove they are scientists.

> Skip the hard questions, and answer the easy ones first.

2. All but one of these are part of the scientific method. Which one is not?
   A. recording data
   B. experimenting
   C. wearing goggles
   D. drawing conclusions

3. Scientists state their guesses as
   A. a theory.
   B. a hypothesis.
   C. a conclusion.
   D. a guess.

4. How are the items in the picture to the right alike?
   A. They all need energy.
   B. They all grow and change.
   C. They all respond to their environment.
   D. All of the above

Name: _____ Date: _____

Lesson One: Process and Inquiry (cont.)

5. Which of the following is not a living thing?
    A. dandelion
    B. lion
    C. baseball bat
    D. spider

Think twice before changing an answer.

6. Which of the following can you hear?
    A. a butterfly flying
    B. a mosquito landing
    C. a cloud floating
    D. the sun setting

7. Animals can do all but which one?
    A. communicate
    B. reproduce
    C. move on their own
    D. make their own food

8. Look at the group below. Choose the one that does not belong.

    elephant, zebra, carrot, giraffe, lion

    A. carrot
    B. lion
    C. elephant
    D. zebra

9. Look at the jars below. Which jar will lose water faster to evaporation?

A.
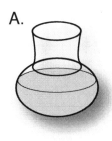

B.

C.
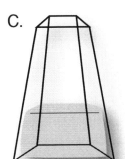

D.
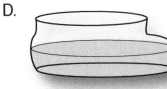

Name: _____ Date: _____

Lesson One: Process and Inquiry (cont.)

10. When matter changes from a gas to a liquid, it is called
    A. evaporation.
    B. condensation.
    C. freezing.
    D. melting.

11. Which of these conclusions can you draw from the data on this graph?
    A. the more peas, the more pods
    B. the shorter the pod, the more peas
    C. the longer the pod, the more peas
    D. the more pods, the more peas

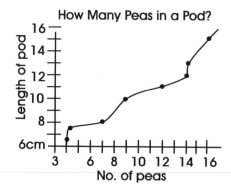

How Many Peas in a Pod?

12. Which of these conclusions could you draw from the data in this table?
    A. the longer time spent brushing, the greater number of teeth cleaned
    B. the greater number of teeth, the longer you have to brush
    C. the longer time spent brushing, the cleaner the teeth
    D. the shorter time spent brushing, the better

Data Table

Name	Time Spent Brushing	No. of Clean Teeth
Devin	1 min.	15
Whitney	3 min.	30
Kibibi	30 sec.	10
Mei	2.5 min.	25

13. Look at the phases of the moon below. What comes next in the sequence?

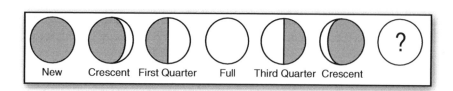

New   Crescent   First Quarter   Full   Third Quarter   Crescent

Pay close attention to how the questions are written.

A.   B.   C.   D.

Name: _____   Date: _____

Lesson One: Process and Inquiry (cont.)

14. What will happen to the temperature in the thermometer if you put ice cubes in cup 1?
    A. The temperature will go up.
    B. The temperature will go down.
    C. The temperature will stay the same.
    D. The temperature will break the thermometer.

15. What would happen if you added hot water to cup 2?
    A. The temperature will go up.
    B. The temperature will go down.
    C. The temperature will stay the same.
    D. The temperature will break the thermometer.

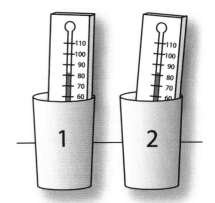

Directions:
Use the picture below to answer questions #16–18. The picture shows a mixture of salt and sand being poured into a container of water.

---

16. Looking at the picture to the right, what do you predict will happen?
    A. The salt will sink.
    B. The sand will sink.
    C. The sand and some of the salt will sink.
    D. Nothing will sink.

17. Looking at the picture, what do you predict will happen?
    A. The sand will float.
    B. The sand and salt will float.
    C. The sand will sink, and the salt will float.
    D. Nothing will float.

18. What will happen to the salt if the water evaporates?
    A. It will evaporate too.
    B. It will remain in the glass.
    C. It will mix with the sand.
    D. It will erode the sand.

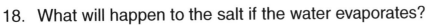

Name: _____ Date: _____

Lesson One: Process and Inquiry (cont.)

19. Using the apple as a model of the earth, what does the skin of the apple represent?
    - A.   the earth's crust
    - B.   the earth's inner core
    - C.   the earth's outer core
    - D.   the earth's mantle

20. What surrounds the earth's inner core?
    - A.   the earth's crust
    - B.   the earth's inner core
    - C.   the earth's outer core
    - D.   the earth's mantle

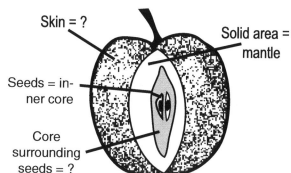

Answer all questions.

Review

1.   Skip the hard questions, and answer the easy ones first.
2.   Think twice before changing an answer.
3.   Pay close attention to how the questions are worded.
4.   Answer all questions.

Name: _____ Date: _____

UNIT FOUR: SCIENCE

Lesson Two: Concepts

Directions:
Choose the best answer for each question.

Use logical reasoning to answer the questions.

1. Which of these is not an organism?
   A. spider
   B. robot
   C. rose
   D. butterfly

2. Which animal is highest on this food chain?
   A. grasshopper
   B. snake
   C. hawk
   D. frog

3. Which animal eats the frog?
   A. grasshopper
   B. snake
   C. hawk
   D. frog

4. How do the cells in your body help you to grow?
   A. The cells in your body grow and split.
   B. Your cells store food for energy.
   C. All cells grow to a certain size.
   D. Your body is made up of millions of cells.

5. Which of these is an example of adaptation?
   A. Rosebushes have thorns.
   B. Sharks often eat smaller fish.
   C. Spiders eat insects.
   D. Hawks' keen eyes help them to find food.

Read each question carefully. All choices may be <u>true</u> but are not the answer to the question.

Name: _____ Date: _____

Lesson Two: Concepts (cont.)

6. Organisms have special defenses that help protect them from harm. Which of these is not a defense mechanism?
   A. camouflage
   B. mimicry
   C. feathers
   D. sharp spines

7. Which of the following lives in habitat *a*?

a.    b.    c.    d.

   A. daisies   B. squirrels   C. frogs   D. bees

8. Which of the following lives in habitat *b*?

   A. daisies   B. squirrels   C. frogs   D. bees

9. How can food change population sizes?
   A. Populations cannot be changed by food.
   B. Populations grow when there is a lot of food.
   C. Populations shrink when there is a lot of food.
   D. Populations remain the same despite the availability of food.

10. Which of these is an endangered animal?
   A. sea otter
   B. dragon
   C. dinosaur
   D. dodo bird

Pay close attention to how the question is worded.

Name: _____   Date: _____

Lesson Two: Concepts (cont.)

11. Look at the drawings. Which one shows a chemical change?

A.    B.    C.    D.

12. Which physical change below does not involve a change in the state of matter?

A.    B.    C.    D.

13. All matter is made up of tiny bits called
    A. volume.
    B. atoms.
    C. molecules.
    D. mass.

14. Look at the pictures. Choose the one not doing work.

A.    B.    C.    D.

Use the process of elimination to find answers.

Name: _____ Date: _____

Lesson Two: Concepts (cont.)

15. Which of the following is an example of a simple machine?

A.  B.  C.  D.

16. A force that slows down objects is

   A. gravity.   B. friction.   C. magnetism.   D. forces.

17. In the space shuttle, what happens to the energy stored in the rocket?

   A. It changes form.
   B. It disappears.
   C. It flows into the air.
   D. It collapses.

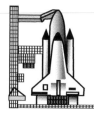

18. Which drawing shows the person not using electricity?

A.  B.  C.  D.

19. Water, wind, and temperature changes are causes of
   A. fossilization.
   B. weathering.
   C. runoff.
   D. glaciers.

Name: _____ Date: _____

Lesson Two: Concepts (cont.)

20. The process of rock wearing away and breaking into small bits is

     A.   erosion.
     B.   fossilization.
     C.   runoff.
     D.   glaciers.

21. Look at the diagram of the elements in the earth's crust. Using the diagram, which element makes up most of the crust?

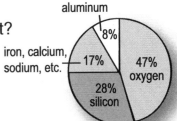
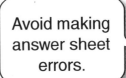

     A.   silicon
     B.   oxygen
     C.   aluminum
     D.   calcium

22. Which of these is not a kind of rock?

     A.   igneous
     B.   sedimentary
     C.   metamorphic
     D.   gem

> Avoid making answer sheet errors.

23. Look at the diagram of the water cycle at the right. Which statement is true about the water cycle?

     A.   It can never rain everywhere in the world at the same time.
     B.   If rain is falling in one place, water is falling in another place.
     C.   It rains more where there is more water.
     D.   It rains when the clouds are condensing.

24. Look at the table of weather data. What term belongs in *a*?

     A.   hail
     B.   sleet
     C.   snow
     D.   rain

Forming inside clouds	Temperature below clouds	Type of precipitation
Drops of water	15°C	a
Ice crystals	0°C	b
Drops of water	0°C	c
Balls of ice	25°C	d

0°C = 32°F

Name: _____ Date: _____

Lesson Two: Concepts (cont.)

25. In the same table, what word belongs in *c*?

    A.   hail   C.   snow
    B.   sleet   D.   rain

26. What causes thunder?

    A.   shock waves
    B.   pressure
    C.   lightning
    D.   rain

27. Using the chart on "Ways to Conserve Water," which activity saves the most water?

    A.   a
    B.   b
    C.   c
    D.   d

Ways to Conserve Water	
Activity	**Amount of water saved**
a. Fill the bathtub halfway instead of full.	68 liters
b. Sweep sidewalks instead of hosing them down.	38 liters per min.
c. Throw trash in a wastebasket, not down the toilet.	19 liters per flush
d. Do not let the water run when you brush your teeth.	15 liters

28. Look at the diagram of the sun and planets below right. What is the correct term for the movement in *a*?
    A.   rotate
    B.   revolve
    C.   orbit
    D.   asteroid

29. What is the correct term for the movement in *c*?
    A.   rotate
    B.   revolve
    C.   orbit
    D.   asteroid

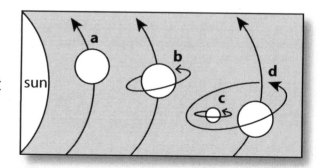

Name: _____　Date: _____

Lesson Two: Concepts (cont.)

> **Directions:**
>
> Use the diagram of the solar system to answer questions #30–35.

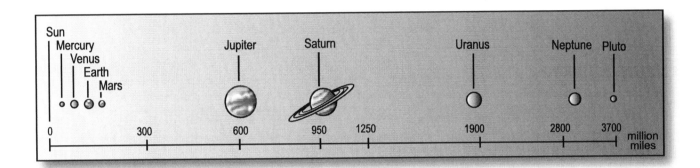

30. Which of these statements is not true for the planet Mars?
　　A.　Mars is the fourth planet from the sun.
　　B.　Water covers most of the surface of Mars.
　　C.　Mars has two moons.
　　D.　Mars is a red, rocky planet.

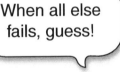

When all else fails, guess!

31. Which is the largest planet?
　　A.　Pluto　　　B.　Jupiter　　　C.　Mercury　　　D.　Venus

32. Which is the coldest planet?
　　A.　Pluto　　　B.　Jupiter　　　C.　Mercury　　　D.　Venus

33. Which planet is the slowest to revolve around the sun?
　　A.　Pluto　　　B.　Jupiter　　　C.　Mercury　　　D.　Venus

34. Which planet is the fastest-moving planet?
　　A.　Pluto　　　B.　Jupiter　　　C.　Mercury　　　D.　Venus

35. Which planet is closest to the sun?
　　A.　Pluto　　　B.　Jupiter　　　C.　Mercury　　　D.　Venus

36. The United States and 15 other countries have cooperated in building the
　　A.　*Mir* Space Station.　　　C.　International Space Station.
　　B.　*Challenger* Space Shuttle.　　　D.　Hubble Space Telescope.

Name: _____ Date: _____

Lesson Two: Concepts (cont.)

37. When food is eaten, it goes through the
    A. circulatory system.
    B. digestive system.
    C. nervous system.
    D. muscular system.

38. Which drawing shows what happens to your food once it leaves your stomach?

    A.   B.    C. 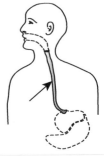   D.

39. The food that doesn't get digested moves into
    A. A.
    B. B.
    C. C.
    D. D.

Directions:
Use the graphs below to answer questions #40–42.

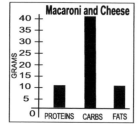
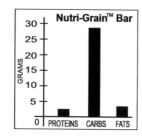
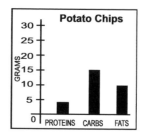
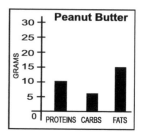

Name: _____   Date: _____

Lesson Two: Concepts (cont.)

40. Jan is on a high-protein, low-carbohydrate diet. Which of the foods should she choose for a snack?
    A. potato chips
    B. Nutri-Grain™ bar
    C. macaroni and cheese
    D. peanut butter

41. Which snack has the most empty carbs?
    A. potato chips
    B. Nutri-Grain™ bar
    C. macaroni and cheese
    D. peanut butter

42. If you wanted to store a lot of energy for the cold weather, which snack should you choose?
    A. potato chips
    B. Nutri-Grain™ bar
    C. macaroni and cheese
    D. peanut butter

43. Junk food should not be eaten often because
    A. it's not a food group.
    B. it does not give your body energy.
    C. it contains too much salt, sugar, or fat.
    D. it gives your body too much energy.

44. Vitamins and minerals help your body to use
    A. proteins.
    B. carbohydrates.
    C. fats.
    D. all of the above.

45. Which of the following will not do serious damage to your body?
    A. drugs
    B. alcohol
    C. oranges
    D. tobacco

Name: _____ Date: _____

Lesson Two: Concepts (cont.)

Review

1. Use logical reasoning to answer the questions.

2. Read each question carefully. All choices may be <u>true</u> but are not the answer to the question.

3. Pay close attention to how the question is worded.

4. Use the process of elimination to find answers.

5. Avoid making answer sheet errors.

6. When all else fails, guess!

Helpful Social Studies Strategies

Test Tips

1. Control your test anxiety. Take deep breaths to calm your nervous energy.
2. Don't panic.
3. Stay calm and focus on the task at hand.
4. Consider every answer choice.
5. Read all answer choices. There may be a better answer farther down the list.

Social Studies Strategies

★　Read each question carefully. Know what you are being asked.

★　Use your time wisely. Answer the ones you know first, and then go back and do the hard ones.

★　Be careful about answer changes. Your first guess is usually correct.

★　Don't over-analyze the answers. It could tie you up in knots.

★　Reread questions and identify the key word or words.

★　Watch out for tricky questions.

★　Read maps, graphs, tables, and data charts carefully.

Name: _____   Date: _____

UNIT FIVE: SOCIAL STUDIES

Lesson One: History and Culture

Stay calm and focus on the task at hand.

Directions:
Choose the best answer for each question.

1. Which of these is the flag of the United States?

A.    B.    C.    D.

2. Which of these is a symbol of Christianity?

A.    B.    C.   D.

3. Which of these is a symbol of Islam?

A.    B.    C.    D.

4. Which of these signs means there is a school nearby?

A.    B.    C.    D.

Name: _____ Date: _____

Lesson One: History and Culture (cont.)

5. Which of these songs is our National Anthem?

     A. "My Country 'Tis of Thee"
     B. "It's a Grand Ole Flag"
     C. "The Star-Spangled Banner"
     D. "America the Beautiful"

Control any test anxiety by taking two deep breaths.

6. Which of these holidays is celebrated in every country of the world, although on different days and in different ways?

     A. Labor Day
     B. New Year's Day
     C. Thanksgiving
     D. Kwanzaa

7. Which of the following is a symbol of freedom?

     A.    B.    C.     D.

8. Which of these sports is usually played in summertime?

     A. football   C. hockey
     B. basketball   D. baseball

9. Which picture shows a monument to the men and women who died in the Vietnam War?

     A.    B.    C.    D.

Name: _____ Date: _____

Lesson One: History and Culture (cont.)

10. Which famous American leader fought for the civil rights of <u>all</u> Americans?

    A.   Richard M. Nixon
    B.   John F. Kennedy
    C.   Martin Luther King, Jr.
    D.   Mahatma Ghandi

11. Which one of these historical landmarks is located in New York City?

    A.   The Eiffel Tower
    B.   Golden Gate Bridge
    C.   Empire State Building
    D.   Mt. Rushmore

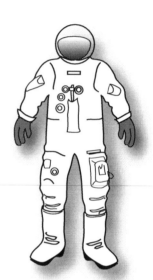

12. Why do immigrants come to the United States?

    A.   To visit Disney World
    B.   To live a better life
    C.   To visit relatives
    D.   To escape paying taxes

13. In 1969, which American astronaut became the first person to walk on the moon?

    A.   Neil Armstrong
    B.   L.L. Cool J
    C.   Jack Nicholson
    D.   Sally Ride

14. What tragic event happened on September 11, 2001?

    A.   Martin Luther King, Jr., was assassinated.
    B.   The Persian Gulf War began.
    C.   Hijacked jets crashed into the World Trade Center.
    D.   The space shuttle *Columbia* exploded.

Eliminate those answers you <u>know</u> are wrong.

15. Which city is the capital of the United States?

    A.   New York
    B.   San Francisco
    C.   Boston
    D.   Washington, D.C.

Name: _____ Date: _____

Lesson One: History and Culture (cont.)

16. Whose face is on a penny?

Consider every answer choice.

   A.   Abraham Lincoln
   B.   Thomas Jefferson
   C.   George Washington
   D.   Benjamin Franklin

17. In what year did the United States become a country?

   A.   1976
   B.   1876
   C.   1776
   D.   1676

18. Who were the first people to live in what is now the United States?

   A.   the English settlers
   B.   the French explorers
   C.   the Roman centurions
   D.   the American Indians

19. Who is Sally Ride?

   A.   first U.S. woman physician
   B.   first U.S. woman to win three gold medals in the Olympics
   C.   first U.S. woman astronaut
   D.   first U.S. woman in Congress

20. Which of these state names is <u>not</u> from an American Indian word?

   A.   Pennsylvania
   B.   Oklahoma
   C.   Ohio
   D.   North Dakota

21. What language is spoken by the most people through-out the world?

Don't over-analyze your answer choices.

   A.   Chinese
   B.   English
   C.   Spanish
   D.   Russian

Name: _____ Date: _____

Lesson One: History and Culture (cont.)

22. Which of these is the largest country in the world?

    A. Canada
    B. Russia
    C. China
    D. United States

23. Who was Mother Teresa?

    A. an Indian princess who saved John Smith
    B. a missionary who worked with the poor of Calcutta, India
    C. an influential politician from India
    D. a Mayan Indian who fought for the rights of her people

24. Where is the Taj Mahal located?

    A. Paris, France
    B. Tokyo, Japan
    C. Agra, India
    D. Pisa, Italy

25. What do historians study?

    A. fossils and rocks
    B. how/why people migrate
    C. people and events of the past
    D. the use of money, goods, and services

Review

1. Stay calm and focus on the task at hand.

2. Control any test anxiety by taking two deep breaths.

3. Consider every answer choice.

4. Don't over-analyze the answer choices.

5. Use the process of elimination.

Name: _____   Date: _____

UNIT FIVE: SOCIAL STUDIES

Lesson Two: Civics, Government, and Economics

Directions:
Choose the best answer for each question.

---

1. Which one of these men was the 43rd President of the United States?

    A.   Jimmy Carter
    B.   George Washington
    C.   Thomas Jefferson
    D.   George W. Bush

2. Who makes the laws in our country?

    A.   the Supreme Court
    B.   the Congress
    C.   the President
    D.   the Principal

Use logical reasoning to choose the best answer.

3. Who makes sure that no law or action violates the U.S. Constitution?

    A.   the Supreme Court
    B.   the Congress
    C.   the President
    D.   the Principal

4. Which one of these first ladies was married to the first U.S. President?

    A.   Laura Bush
    B.   Barbara Bush
    C.   Martha Washington
    D.   Dolley Madison

Name: _____ Date: _____

Lesson Two: Civics, Government, and Economics (cont.)

5. Why does the government collect taxes from people?
    A.   to pay for services like roads, libraries, schools, etc.
    B.   to pay the bank for making money
    C.   to encourage people to work harder
    D.   to make people obey the laws

6. Which one of these is the leader of a city or town?

    A.   mayor
    B.   governor
    C.   president
    D.   king

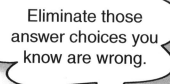
Eliminate those answer choices you know are wrong.

7. Which one of these is the leader of a state?

    A.   mayor
    B.   governor
    C.   president
    D.   king

8. Who wrote the Declaration of Independence?

    A.   Abraham Lincoln
    B.   William Jefferson Clinton
    C.   Thomas Jefferson
    D.   George Washington

9. What is the Constitution of the United States?

    A.   a collection of rights for citizens
    B.   a list of reasons the colonies wanted independence
    C.   the basic laws and principles of our country
    D.   a law that sets the voting age at 18

10. Why do cities have laws?

    A.   to collect taxes from people
    B.   to make the police more powerful
    C.   to help people live together
    D.   to give people jobs

Name: _____ Date: _____

Lesson Two: Civics, Government, and Economics (cont.)

11. What does it mean to be a citizen?

    A.   You get a passport.
    B.   You have to stay in that country.
    C.   You are a legal member of that country.
    D.   You have to work in that country and pay taxes.

> Reread the question. What are the key words?

12. Important characteristics of citizenship include all but which one?

    A.   a person can vote
    B.   a person must pay taxes
    C.   a person gets free food
    D.   a person receives protection from the government

13. What are some important rights that citizens have?

    A.   to choose your own friends
    B.   to believe what you want to believe
    C.   to express your opinion safely
    D.   All of these are rights.

14. What is the most important responsibility of an American citizen?

    A.   to get educated
    B.   to support your family
    C.   to obey the laws
    D.   none of these

> Read all answer choices after you find the answer. "All of these" or "none of these" may be a better answer.

15. Diversity is an important value of our country. What does *diversity* mean?

    A.   appreciating the patriotism of our neighbors
    B.   appreciating the friendliness of our neighbors
    C.   appreciating the differences and variety of our neighbors
    D.   appreciating the honesty of our neighbors

Name: _____ Date: _____

Lesson Two: Civics, Government, and Economics (cont.)

16. How do citizens of the United States select their leaders?

    A.   They vote.
    B.   They draw names out of a hat.
    C.   They let the President choose.
    D.   none of these

17. Which is an example of a good citizen?

    A.   students who throw trash from a car
    B.   students who live in a small town
    C.   students who cross the street at the crosswalk
    D.   students whose parents pay a lot of taxes

18. Which of these is the commander-in-chief of the military?

    A.   the president
    B.   the vice president
    C.   the Congress
    D.   the Senate

> Watch out for tricky language. Identify the <u>key</u> word or words.

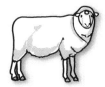

19. Where does the government get the money to pay for the services it gives its citizens?

    A.   from the bank
    B.   from taxes that people pay
    C.   from campaign money
    D.   from an ATM machine

20. Who takes over the government if something happens to the president?

    A.   the first lady   C.   the vice president
    B.   the last president   D.   the governor

21. Which one of these is not a producer?

    A.    B.   C.   D.

Name: _____ Date: _____

Lesson Two: Civics, Government, and Economics (cont.)

22. Which one of these represents a <u>durable good</u> that consumers consume?

A.    B.    C.    D.

23. Which one of these represents a <u>perishable good</u> that consumers consume?

A.    B.    C.    D.

24. Which one of these shows a person who provides a service?

A.    B.    C.    D.

25. Which of these is found in most communities?

    A.   museum
    B.   ice rink
    C.   grocery store
    D.   airport

26. What does a factory worker do?

    A.   fixes things
    B.   invents things
    C.   sells things
    D.   makes things

Name: _____   Date: _____

Lesson Two: Civics, Government, and Economics (cont.)

27. Which of these is a crop that grows best on a California or Florida farm?

    A.   wheat
    B.   strawberries
    C.   soybeans
    D.   corn

28. Where are the suburbs located?

    A.   around big cities
    B.   on midwestern farms
    C.   in France or Spain
    D.   in the coal mines of Pennsylvania

29. Which of the people in the pictures below would most likely be a volunteer?

A.  B.  C.  D.

30. Which of these is public property?

A.  B.  C.  D.

Review

1. Use logical reasoning to choose the best answers.
2. Use the process of elimination.
3. Reread questions. Identify the <u>key</u> word or words.
4. Read all answer choices after you find the answer. "All of these" or "none of these" may be a better answer.
5. Watch out for tricky language. Know what the question is asking.

Name: _____   Date: _____

UNIT FIVE: SOCIAL STUDIES

Lesson Three: Geography

Directions:
Choose the best answer for each question.

1. Which of these is a desert?

   A. Panama
   B. Missouri
   C. Sahara
   D. Indonesia

2. Which of these is <u>not</u> a river?

   A. Nile
   B. Amazon
   C. Mississippi
   D. Everest

3. Where is Vatican City?

   A. Rome
   B. Beijing
   C. New York
   D. Los Angeles

4. In what country is *Big Ben* located?

   A. China
   B. Italy
   C. England
   D. United States

5. Choose the picture that shows a compass rose.

A.   B.   C.   D.

Take a deep breath and stay calm. Don't panic.

Name: _____ Date: _____

Lesson Three: Geography (cont.)

Directions:
Use the map of the United States for questions #6–12.

6. In which direction would you travel if you wanted to get from Massachusetts to California?

   A.   north
   B.   south
   C.   east
   D.   west

7. In which direction would you have to travel to get from Kansas to Ohio?

   A.   north
   B.   south
   C.   east
   D.   west

Name: _____ Date: _____

Lesson Three: Geography (cont.)

8. In which direction would you have to travel to get from Florida to Michigan?

    A.   north
    B.   south
    C.   east
    D.   west

9. In which direction would you travel to get from Texas to New York?

    A.   northwest
    B.   south
    C.   northeast
    D.   west

10. All but one of these are on maps. Which one isn't?

    A.   compass rose
    B.   map key
    C.   mile key
    D.   tree key

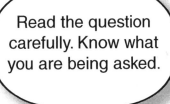

Read the question carefully. Know what you are being asked.

11. Which one of these states is in the eastern United States?

    A.   Wyoming
    B.   Missouri
    C.   Alaska
    D.   Rhode Island

12. Which one of these states is <u>not</u> a southern state?

    A.   Wisconsin
    B.   Mississippi
    C.   Alabama
    D.   Georgia

Name: _____ Date: _____

Lesson Three: Geography (cont.)

Directions:
Use the world map for questions #13–16.

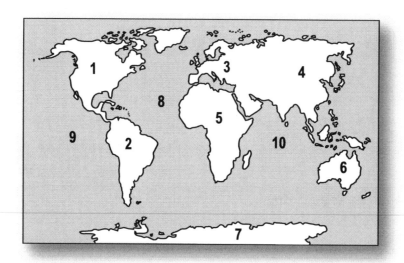

13. What continent is numbered 2?

A. North America
B. South America
C. Africa
D. Asia

Use time wisely. Don't spend too much time on any one question.

14. Which country is numbered 6?

A. Africa
B. New Zealand
C. Indonesia
D. Australia

15. What is the name of the ocean numbered 8?

A. Atlantic
B. Pacific
C. Indian
D. Arctic

16. Which of these is the largest ocean?

A. Atlantic
B. Pacific
C. Indian
D. Arctic

Name: _____ Date: _____

Lesson Three: Geography (cont.)

> **Directions:**
> Use the town map below to answer questions #17–20.

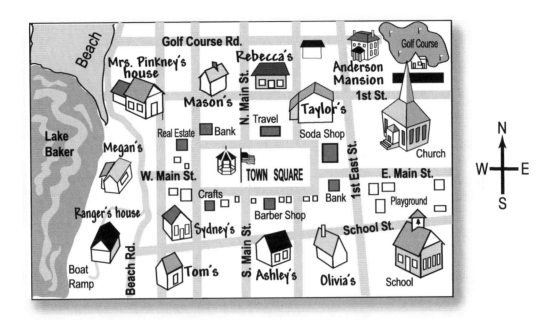

17. Which of these is farthest from the school?
    A. Ashley's house   C. Taylor's house
    B. Tom's house   D. the church

18. If Megan wanted to walk from her house to the town square, which street would she take for the shortest route?
    A. South Main Street
    B. North Main Street
    C. East Main Street
    D. West Main Street

19. Who has the shortest walk to the beach?
    A. Mason   C. Taylor
    B. Sydney   D. Megan

20. Olivia took the shortest route from her house to the golf course where she worked. What building did she pass on her right?
    A. the soda shop   C. the church
    B. the bank   D. Taylor's house

Name: _____ Date: _____

Lesson Three: Geography (cont.)

Directions:
Use the road map to answer questions #21–25.

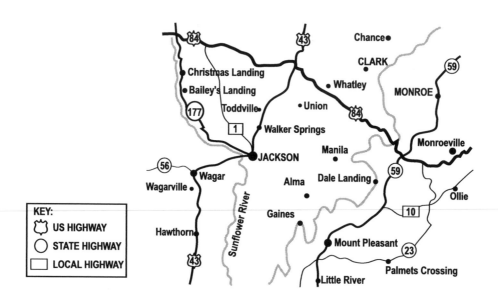

21. If I live in Whatley and wanted to go to Christmas Landing, which of these would I take?
    A. U.S. highway
    B. state highway
    C. local highway
    D. both A and B

22. Sunflower River is between which two U.S. highways?
    A. 84 and 177
    B. 69 and 177
    C. 43 and 84
    D. 10 and 21

23. Which town is the farthest west on this map?
    A. Chance
    B. Wagarville
    C. Dale Landing
    D. Hawthorn

24. Which city probably has the most people?
    A. Manila
    B. Monroeville
    C. Jackson
    D. Little River

25. If you lived in Ollie, in which direction would you travel to get to Little River?
    A. north
    B. southwest
    C. northeast
    D. west

Name: _____   Date: _____

Lesson Three: Geography (cont.)

Directions:
For items #26–30, use the map below.

---

26. Which of these is labeled #2 on the map?

    A.   mountain
    B.   volcano
    C.   hill
    D.   plateau

27. Which of these is labeled #9 on the map?

    A.   waterfall
    B.   beach
    C.   desert
    D.   prairie

28. Which of these is labeled #5 on the map?

    A.   swamp
    B.   beach
    C.   caves
    D.   mountain

29. What is the number of the lake?

    A.   8
    B.   1
    C.   7
    D.   10

30. What is the number of the harbor?

    A.   8
    B.   1
    C.   7
    D.   10

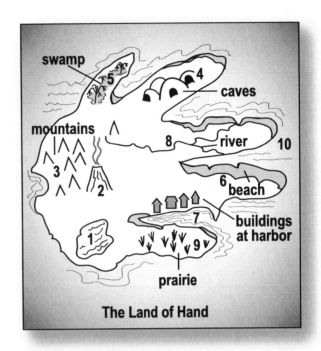

The Land of Hand

Be careful of changing answers. Your first guess is usually the best.

Name: _____ Date: _____

Lesson Three: Geography (cont.)

Directions:
Use the illustrations of a globe to answer questions #31–35.

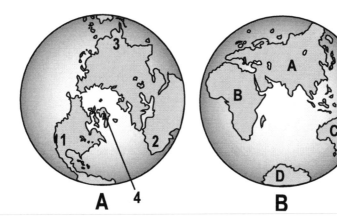

A   B

31. Which hemisphere is shown in Figure A?

    A.   Northern
    B.   Southern
    C.   Eastern
    D.   Western

When the questions sound complicated, read them again or try to put them in your own words.

32. Which hemisphere is shown in Figure B?

    A.   Northern
    B.   Southern
    C.   Eastern
    D.   Western

33. If a person lives at each letter, A through D, on Figure B, which one would have the warmest weather?

    A.   D
    B.   C
    C.   B
    D.   A

Name: _____ Date: _____

Lesson Three: Geography (cont.)

34. Which person would have the easiest chance to visit the beach?

    A.   D
    B.   C
    C.   B
    D.   A

35. If a person lives at each number, 1 through 4, on Figure A, which one would have the coldest weather?

    A.   1
    B.   2
    C.   3
    D.   4

Review

1. Take a deep breath and stay calm. Don't panic.

2. Read the question carefully. Know what you are being asked.

3. Use time wisely. Don't spend too much time on any one question.

4. Be careful of changing answers. Your first guess is usually the best.

5. When the questions sound complicated, read them again or try to put them in your own words.

Name: _____ Date: _____

Standardized Testing Grade 3 Answer Sheet

School:	Student Name		
Teacher:	Last	First	MI
Female ○ Male ○			

Birth Date

Month	Day	Year
Jan ○	⓪ ⓪	⓪ ⓪
Feb ○	① ①	① ①
Mar ○	② ②	② ②
Apr ○	③ ③	③ ③
May ○	④	④ ④
Jun ○	⑤	⑤ ⑤
Jul ○	⑥	⑥ ⑥
Aug ○	⑦	⑦ ⑦
Sep ○	⑧	⑧ ⑧
Oct ○	⑨	⑨ ⑨
Nov ○		
Dec ○		

Grade ③ ④ ⑤ ⑥ ⑦ ⑧

(Student name grid: columns of bubbles ○ A B C D E F G H I J K L M N O P Q R S T U V W X Y Z)

Unit One: Reading   Lesson One: Vocabulary

1. Ⓐ Ⓑ Ⓒ Ⓓ	9. Ⓐ Ⓑ Ⓒ Ⓓ	17. Ⓐ Ⓑ Ⓒ Ⓓ	25. Ⓐ Ⓑ Ⓒ Ⓓ	33. Ⓐ Ⓑ Ⓒ Ⓓ
2. Ⓐ Ⓑ Ⓒ Ⓓ	10. Ⓐ Ⓑ Ⓒ Ⓓ	18. Ⓐ Ⓑ Ⓒ Ⓓ	26. Ⓐ Ⓑ Ⓒ Ⓓ	34. Ⓐ Ⓑ Ⓒ Ⓓ
3. Ⓐ Ⓑ Ⓒ Ⓓ	11. Ⓐ Ⓑ Ⓒ Ⓓ	19. Ⓐ Ⓑ Ⓒ Ⓓ	27. Ⓐ Ⓑ Ⓒ Ⓓ	35. Ⓐ Ⓑ Ⓒ Ⓓ
4. Ⓐ Ⓑ Ⓒ Ⓓ	12. Ⓐ Ⓑ Ⓒ Ⓓ	20. Ⓐ Ⓑ Ⓒ Ⓓ	28. Ⓐ Ⓑ Ⓒ Ⓓ	36. Ⓐ Ⓑ Ⓒ Ⓓ
5. Ⓐ Ⓑ Ⓒ Ⓓ	13. Ⓐ Ⓑ Ⓒ Ⓓ	21. Ⓐ Ⓑ Ⓒ Ⓓ	29. Ⓐ Ⓑ Ⓒ Ⓓ	37. Ⓐ Ⓑ Ⓒ Ⓓ
6. Ⓐ Ⓑ Ⓒ Ⓓ	14. Ⓐ Ⓑ Ⓒ Ⓓ	22. Ⓐ Ⓑ Ⓒ Ⓓ	30. Ⓐ Ⓑ Ⓒ Ⓓ	38. Ⓐ Ⓑ Ⓒ Ⓓ
7. Ⓐ Ⓑ Ⓒ Ⓓ	15. Ⓐ Ⓑ Ⓒ Ⓓ	23. Ⓐ Ⓑ Ⓒ Ⓓ	31. Ⓐ Ⓑ Ⓒ Ⓓ	39. Ⓐ Ⓑ Ⓒ Ⓓ
8. Ⓐ Ⓑ Ⓒ Ⓓ	16. Ⓐ Ⓑ Ⓒ Ⓓ	24. Ⓐ Ⓑ Ⓒ Ⓓ	32. Ⓐ Ⓑ Ⓒ Ⓓ	40. Ⓐ Ⓑ Ⓒ Ⓓ

Name: _____   Date: _____

Standardized Testing Grade 3 Answer Sheet

Unit One: Reading   Lesson Two: Word Analysis

1. Ⓐ Ⓑ Ⓒ Ⓓ	7. Ⓐ Ⓑ Ⓒ Ⓓ	13. Ⓐ Ⓑ Ⓒ Ⓓ	19. Ⓐ Ⓑ Ⓒ Ⓓ	25. Ⓐ Ⓑ Ⓒ Ⓓ
2. Ⓐ Ⓑ Ⓒ Ⓓ	8. Ⓐ Ⓑ Ⓒ Ⓓ	14. Ⓐ Ⓑ Ⓒ Ⓓ	20. Ⓐ Ⓑ Ⓒ Ⓓ	26. Ⓐ Ⓑ Ⓒ Ⓓ
3. Ⓐ Ⓑ Ⓒ Ⓓ	9. Ⓐ Ⓑ Ⓒ Ⓓ	15. Ⓐ Ⓑ Ⓒ Ⓓ	21. Ⓐ Ⓑ Ⓒ Ⓓ	
4. Ⓐ Ⓑ Ⓒ Ⓓ	10. Ⓐ Ⓑ Ⓒ Ⓓ	16. Ⓐ Ⓑ Ⓒ Ⓓ	22. Ⓐ Ⓑ Ⓒ Ⓓ	
5. Ⓐ Ⓑ Ⓒ Ⓓ	11. Ⓐ Ⓑ Ⓒ Ⓓ	17. Ⓐ Ⓑ Ⓒ Ⓓ	23. Ⓐ Ⓑ Ⓒ Ⓓ	
6. Ⓐ Ⓑ Ⓒ Ⓓ	12. Ⓐ Ⓑ Ⓒ Ⓓ	18. Ⓐ Ⓑ Ⓒ Ⓓ	24. Ⓐ Ⓑ Ⓒ Ⓓ	

Unit One: Reading   Lesson Three: Reading Comprehension

1. Ⓐ Ⓑ Ⓒ Ⓓ	6. Ⓐ Ⓑ Ⓒ Ⓓ	11. Ⓐ Ⓑ Ⓒ Ⓓ	16. Ⓐ Ⓑ Ⓒ Ⓓ	21. Ⓐ Ⓑ Ⓒ Ⓓ
2. Ⓐ Ⓑ Ⓒ Ⓓ	7. Ⓐ Ⓑ Ⓒ Ⓓ	12. Ⓐ Ⓑ Ⓒ Ⓓ	17. Ⓐ Ⓑ Ⓒ Ⓓ	22. Ⓐ Ⓑ Ⓒ Ⓓ
3. Ⓐ Ⓑ Ⓒ Ⓓ	8. Ⓐ Ⓑ Ⓒ Ⓓ	13. Ⓐ Ⓑ Ⓒ Ⓓ	18. Ⓐ Ⓑ Ⓒ Ⓓ	23. Ⓐ Ⓑ Ⓒ Ⓓ
4. Ⓐ Ⓑ Ⓒ Ⓓ	9. Ⓐ Ⓑ Ⓒ Ⓓ	14. Ⓐ Ⓑ Ⓒ Ⓓ	19. Ⓐ Ⓑ Ⓒ Ⓓ	24. Ⓐ Ⓑ Ⓒ Ⓓ
5. Ⓐ Ⓑ Ⓒ Ⓓ	10. Ⓐ Ⓑ Ⓒ Ⓓ	15. Ⓐ Ⓑ Ⓒ Ⓓ	20. Ⓐ Ⓑ Ⓒ Ⓓ	25. Ⓐ Ⓑ Ⓒ Ⓓ

Unit Two: Language   Lesson One: Mechanics

1. Ⓐ Ⓑ Ⓒ Ⓓ	16. Ⓐ Ⓑ Ⓒ Ⓓ	31. Ⓐ Ⓑ Ⓒ Ⓓ	46. Ⓐ Ⓑ Ⓒ Ⓓ	61. Ⓐ Ⓑ Ⓒ Ⓓ
2. Ⓐ Ⓑ Ⓒ Ⓓ	17. Ⓐ Ⓑ Ⓒ Ⓓ	32. Ⓐ Ⓑ Ⓒ Ⓓ	47. Ⓐ Ⓑ Ⓒ Ⓓ	62. Ⓐ Ⓑ Ⓒ Ⓓ
3. Ⓐ Ⓑ Ⓒ Ⓓ	18. Ⓐ Ⓑ Ⓒ Ⓓ	33. Ⓐ Ⓑ Ⓒ Ⓓ	48. Ⓐ Ⓑ Ⓒ Ⓓ	63. Ⓐ Ⓑ Ⓒ Ⓓ
4. Ⓐ Ⓑ Ⓒ Ⓓ	19. Ⓐ Ⓑ Ⓒ Ⓓ	34. Ⓐ Ⓑ Ⓒ Ⓓ	49. Ⓐ Ⓑ Ⓒ Ⓓ	64. Ⓐ Ⓑ Ⓒ Ⓓ
5. Ⓐ Ⓑ Ⓒ Ⓓ	20. Ⓐ Ⓑ Ⓒ Ⓓ	35. Ⓐ Ⓑ Ⓒ Ⓓ	50. Ⓐ Ⓑ Ⓒ Ⓓ	65. Ⓐ Ⓑ Ⓒ Ⓓ
6. Ⓐ Ⓑ Ⓒ Ⓓ	21. Ⓐ Ⓑ Ⓒ Ⓓ	36. Ⓐ Ⓑ Ⓒ Ⓓ	51. Ⓐ Ⓑ Ⓒ Ⓓ	66. Ⓐ Ⓑ Ⓒ Ⓓ
7. Ⓐ Ⓑ Ⓒ Ⓓ	22. Ⓐ Ⓑ Ⓒ Ⓓ	37. Ⓐ Ⓑ Ⓒ Ⓓ	52. Ⓐ Ⓑ Ⓒ Ⓓ	67. Ⓐ Ⓑ Ⓒ Ⓓ
8. Ⓐ Ⓑ Ⓒ Ⓓ	23. Ⓐ Ⓑ Ⓒ Ⓓ	38. Ⓐ Ⓑ Ⓒ Ⓓ	53. Ⓐ Ⓑ Ⓒ Ⓓ	68. Ⓐ Ⓑ Ⓒ Ⓓ
9. Ⓐ Ⓑ Ⓒ Ⓓ	24. Ⓐ Ⓑ Ⓒ Ⓓ	39. Ⓐ Ⓑ Ⓒ Ⓓ	54. Ⓐ Ⓑ Ⓒ Ⓓ	69. Ⓐ Ⓑ Ⓒ Ⓓ
10. Ⓐ Ⓑ Ⓒ Ⓓ	25. Ⓐ Ⓑ Ⓒ Ⓓ	40. Ⓐ Ⓑ Ⓒ Ⓓ	55. Ⓐ Ⓑ Ⓒ Ⓓ	70. Ⓐ Ⓑ Ⓒ Ⓓ
11. Ⓐ Ⓑ Ⓒ Ⓓ	26. Ⓐ Ⓑ Ⓒ Ⓓ	41. Ⓐ Ⓑ Ⓒ Ⓓ	56. Ⓐ Ⓑ Ⓒ Ⓓ	71. Ⓐ Ⓑ Ⓒ Ⓓ
12. Ⓐ Ⓑ Ⓒ Ⓓ	27. Ⓐ Ⓑ Ⓒ Ⓓ	42. Ⓐ Ⓑ Ⓒ Ⓓ	57. Ⓐ Ⓑ Ⓒ Ⓓ	72. Ⓐ Ⓑ Ⓒ Ⓓ
13. Ⓐ Ⓑ Ⓒ Ⓓ	28. Ⓐ Ⓑ Ⓒ Ⓓ	43. Ⓐ Ⓑ Ⓒ Ⓓ	58. Ⓐ Ⓑ Ⓒ Ⓓ	73. Ⓐ Ⓑ Ⓒ Ⓓ
14. Ⓐ Ⓑ Ⓒ Ⓓ	29. Ⓐ Ⓑ Ⓒ Ⓓ	44. Ⓐ Ⓑ Ⓒ Ⓓ	59. Ⓐ Ⓑ Ⓒ Ⓓ	74. Ⓐ Ⓑ Ⓒ Ⓓ
15. Ⓐ Ⓑ Ⓒ Ⓓ	30. Ⓐ Ⓑ Ⓒ Ⓓ	45. Ⓐ Ⓑ Ⓒ Ⓓ	60. Ⓐ Ⓑ Ⓒ Ⓓ	75. Ⓐ Ⓑ Ⓒ Ⓓ

Name: _____   Date: _____

Standardized Testing Grade 3 Answer Sheet

Unit Two: Language   **Lesson Two: Expression**

1. Ⓐ Ⓑ Ⓒ Ⓓ	11. Ⓐ Ⓑ Ⓒ Ⓓ	21. Ⓐ Ⓑ Ⓒ Ⓓ	31. Ⓐ Ⓑ Ⓒ Ⓓ	41. Ⓐ Ⓑ Ⓒ Ⓓ
2. Ⓐ Ⓑ Ⓒ Ⓓ	12. Ⓐ Ⓑ Ⓒ Ⓓ	22. Ⓐ Ⓑ Ⓒ Ⓓ	32. Ⓐ Ⓑ Ⓒ Ⓓ	42. Ⓐ Ⓑ Ⓒ Ⓓ
3. Ⓐ Ⓑ Ⓒ Ⓓ	13. Ⓐ Ⓑ Ⓒ Ⓓ	23. Ⓐ Ⓑ Ⓒ Ⓓ	33. Ⓐ Ⓑ Ⓒ Ⓓ	43. Ⓐ Ⓑ Ⓒ Ⓓ
4. Ⓐ Ⓑ Ⓒ Ⓓ	14. Ⓐ Ⓑ Ⓒ Ⓓ	24. Ⓐ Ⓑ Ⓒ Ⓓ	34. Ⓐ Ⓑ Ⓒ Ⓓ	44. Ⓐ Ⓑ Ⓒ Ⓓ
5. Ⓐ Ⓑ Ⓒ Ⓓ	15. Ⓐ Ⓑ Ⓒ Ⓓ	25. Ⓐ Ⓑ Ⓒ Ⓓ	35. Ⓐ Ⓑ Ⓒ Ⓓ	45. Ⓐ Ⓑ Ⓒ Ⓓ
6. Ⓐ Ⓑ Ⓒ Ⓓ	16. Ⓐ Ⓑ Ⓒ Ⓓ	26. Ⓐ Ⓑ Ⓒ Ⓓ	36. Ⓐ Ⓑ Ⓒ Ⓓ	46. Ⓐ Ⓑ Ⓒ Ⓓ
7. Ⓐ Ⓑ Ⓒ Ⓓ	17. Ⓐ Ⓑ Ⓒ Ⓓ	27. Ⓐ Ⓑ Ⓒ Ⓓ	37. Ⓐ Ⓑ Ⓒ Ⓓ	47. Ⓐ Ⓑ Ⓒ Ⓓ
8. Ⓐ Ⓑ Ⓒ Ⓓ	18. Ⓐ Ⓑ Ⓒ Ⓓ	28. Ⓐ Ⓑ Ⓒ Ⓓ	38. Ⓐ Ⓑ Ⓒ Ⓓ	48. Ⓐ Ⓑ Ⓒ Ⓓ
9. Ⓐ Ⓑ Ⓒ Ⓓ	19. Ⓐ Ⓑ Ⓒ Ⓓ	29. Ⓐ Ⓑ Ⓒ Ⓓ	39. Ⓐ Ⓑ Ⓒ Ⓓ	49. Ⓐ Ⓑ Ⓒ Ⓓ
10. Ⓐ Ⓑ Ⓒ Ⓓ	20. Ⓐ Ⓑ Ⓒ Ⓓ	30. Ⓐ Ⓑ Ⓒ Ⓓ	40. Ⓐ Ⓑ Ⓒ Ⓓ	50. Ⓐ Ⓑ Ⓒ Ⓓ

Unit Two: Language   **Lesson Three: Information Skills**

1. Ⓐ Ⓑ Ⓒ Ⓓ	9. Ⓐ Ⓑ Ⓒ Ⓓ	17. Ⓐ Ⓑ Ⓒ Ⓓ	25. Ⓐ Ⓑ Ⓒ Ⓓ	33. Ⓐ Ⓑ Ⓒ Ⓓ
2. Ⓐ Ⓑ Ⓒ Ⓓ	10. Ⓐ Ⓑ Ⓒ Ⓓ	18. Ⓐ Ⓑ Ⓒ Ⓓ	26. Ⓐ Ⓑ Ⓒ Ⓓ	34. Ⓐ Ⓑ Ⓒ Ⓓ
3. Ⓐ Ⓑ Ⓒ Ⓓ	11. Ⓐ Ⓑ Ⓒ Ⓓ	19. Ⓐ Ⓑ Ⓒ Ⓓ	27. Ⓐ Ⓑ Ⓒ Ⓓ	35. Ⓐ Ⓑ Ⓒ Ⓓ
4. Ⓐ Ⓑ Ⓒ Ⓓ	12. Ⓐ Ⓑ Ⓒ Ⓓ	20. Ⓐ Ⓑ Ⓒ Ⓓ	28. Ⓐ Ⓑ Ⓒ Ⓓ	36. Ⓐ Ⓑ Ⓒ Ⓓ
5. Ⓐ Ⓑ Ⓒ Ⓓ	13. Ⓐ Ⓑ Ⓒ Ⓓ	21. Ⓐ Ⓑ Ⓒ Ⓓ	29. Ⓐ Ⓑ Ⓒ Ⓓ	37. Ⓐ Ⓑ Ⓒ Ⓓ
6. Ⓐ Ⓑ Ⓒ Ⓓ	14. Ⓐ Ⓑ Ⓒ Ⓓ	22. Ⓐ Ⓑ Ⓒ Ⓓ	30. Ⓐ Ⓑ Ⓒ Ⓓ	38. Ⓐ Ⓑ Ⓒ Ⓓ
7. Ⓐ Ⓑ Ⓒ Ⓓ	15. Ⓐ Ⓑ Ⓒ Ⓓ	23. Ⓐ Ⓑ Ⓒ Ⓓ	31. Ⓐ Ⓑ Ⓒ Ⓓ	39. Ⓐ Ⓑ Ⓒ Ⓓ
8. Ⓐ Ⓑ Ⓒ Ⓓ	16. Ⓐ Ⓑ Ⓒ Ⓓ	24. Ⓐ Ⓑ Ⓒ Ⓓ	32. Ⓐ Ⓑ Ⓒ Ⓓ	40. Ⓐ Ⓑ Ⓒ Ⓓ

Unit Three: Mathematics   **Lesson One: Concepts**

1. Ⓐ Ⓑ Ⓒ Ⓓ	11. Ⓐ Ⓑ Ⓒ Ⓓ	21. Ⓐ Ⓑ Ⓒ Ⓓ	31. Ⓐ Ⓑ Ⓒ Ⓓ	41. Ⓐ Ⓑ Ⓒ Ⓓ
2. Ⓐ Ⓑ Ⓒ Ⓓ	12. Ⓐ Ⓑ Ⓒ Ⓓ	22. Ⓐ Ⓑ Ⓒ Ⓓ	32. Ⓐ Ⓑ Ⓒ Ⓓ	42. Ⓐ Ⓑ Ⓒ Ⓓ
3. Ⓐ Ⓑ Ⓒ Ⓓ	13. Ⓐ Ⓑ Ⓒ Ⓓ	23. Ⓐ Ⓑ Ⓒ Ⓓ	33. Ⓐ Ⓑ Ⓒ Ⓓ	43. Ⓐ Ⓑ Ⓒ Ⓓ
4. Ⓐ Ⓑ Ⓒ Ⓓ	14. Ⓐ Ⓑ Ⓒ Ⓓ	24. Ⓐ Ⓑ Ⓒ Ⓓ	34. Ⓐ Ⓑ Ⓒ Ⓓ	44. Ⓐ Ⓑ Ⓒ Ⓓ
5. Ⓐ Ⓑ Ⓒ Ⓓ	15. Ⓐ Ⓑ Ⓒ Ⓓ	25. Ⓐ Ⓑ Ⓒ Ⓓ	35. Ⓐ Ⓑ Ⓒ Ⓓ	45. Ⓐ Ⓑ Ⓒ Ⓓ
6. Ⓐ Ⓑ Ⓒ Ⓓ	16. Ⓐ Ⓑ Ⓒ Ⓓ	26. Ⓐ Ⓑ Ⓒ Ⓓ	36. Ⓐ Ⓑ Ⓒ Ⓓ	46. Ⓐ Ⓑ Ⓒ Ⓓ
7. Ⓐ Ⓑ Ⓒ Ⓓ	17. Ⓐ Ⓑ Ⓒ Ⓓ	27. Ⓐ Ⓑ Ⓒ Ⓓ	37. Ⓐ Ⓑ Ⓒ Ⓓ	47. Ⓐ Ⓑ Ⓒ Ⓓ
8. Ⓐ Ⓑ Ⓒ Ⓓ	18. Ⓐ Ⓑ Ⓒ Ⓓ	28. Ⓐ Ⓑ Ⓒ Ⓓ	38. Ⓐ Ⓑ Ⓒ Ⓓ	48. Ⓐ Ⓑ Ⓒ Ⓓ
9. Ⓐ Ⓑ Ⓒ Ⓓ	19. Ⓐ Ⓑ Ⓒ Ⓓ	29. Ⓐ Ⓑ Ⓒ Ⓓ	39. Ⓐ Ⓑ Ⓒ Ⓓ	49. Ⓐ Ⓑ Ⓒ Ⓓ
10. Ⓐ Ⓑ Ⓒ Ⓓ	20. Ⓐ Ⓑ Ⓒ Ⓓ	30. Ⓐ Ⓑ Ⓒ Ⓓ	40. Ⓐ Ⓑ Ⓒ Ⓓ	50. Ⓐ Ⓑ Ⓒ Ⓓ

Name: _____ Date: _____

Lesson One: Vocabulary

Directions

This is a test about words and their meanings. For items #1–10, decide which one of the four answers <u>has most nearly the same</u> meaning as the underlined word above it. Then fill in the answer space on your answer sheet that has the same letter as the correct answer.

BE ALERT!
Read the directions carefully. Are you looking for a word that means the same or a word that means the opposite? How do you know?

1. <u>sharp</u> scissors
   A. sudden
   B. pointed
   C. bitter
   D. harsh

2. <u>dangerous</u> roads
   A. hazardous
   B. shaky
   C. safe
   D. escape

5. Her <u>maroon</u> sweater was left at school.
   A. bulky
   B. new
   C. red
   D. old

6. Why did he slide down the <u>bannister</u>?
   A. post
   B. railing
   C. stairs
   D. hill

7. Harry was looking for <u>platform</u> $9\frac{3}{4}$.
   A. landing
   B. stage
   C. plane
   D. train

3. a big <u>grin</u>
   A. smirk
   B. sneer
   C. laugh
   D. smile

4. angry <u>customer</u>
   A. buyer
   B. teacher
   C. man
   D. boxer

BE SMART!
#5–10 represent a _<u>format</u> change, not a change in directions.

Helpful Reading Strategies

Test Tips

★ Read <u>all</u> directions carefully.

★ Be sure you understand the directions.

★ Read <u>all</u> answer choices before choosing one.

★ Format changes do <u>not</u> always signal a change in directions.

★ Look for the key words in the directions.

★ Use the process of elimination to find answers.

Reading Strategies

★ When you are looking for the main idea of a selection, look for the first sentence, the last sentence, or the title. These usually provide a good clue to the main idea.

★ When the directions say, *"according to the selection ...,"* look back at the reading and find the sentence or sentences that provide proof. In your head, highlight that sentence.

★ When the directions say choose the *"most important idea,"* or *"the main problem,"* remember that there is probably more than one right answer. You need to look for the BEST answer.

★ When you are trying to figure out a vocabulary word from context, replace the word with the answer words to see if they fit (like trying on shoes!). You can usually find the right one this way.

★ Watch out for negatives. Some questions say, *"Which of the following **is not true**?"*. That means that three answers are true, and one is false. You are looking for the false one.

Name: _____ Date: _____

H

Lesson One: Vocabulary (cont.)

8. The detective planned to <u>investigate</u> the robbery.
   A. hide
   B. test
   C. ignore
   D. examine

9. To <u>complete</u> is to _____.
   A. finish
   B. start
   C. build
   D. express

10. A <u>bundle</u> is a _____.
   A. crate
   B. bunch
   C. cluster
   D. backpack

BE CAREFUL!
There may be more than one word that is **true**. Remember, you are looking for the word that means the same or nearly the same.

Directions: For #11–15, darken the circle for the word or words that mean the **opposite** of the underlined word.

---

11. the <u>lower</u> floor
   A. basement
   B. upper
   C. ground
   D. fifth

12. a <u>wet</u> umbrella
   A. torn
   B. yellow
   C. dry
   D. little

13. the <u>friendly</u> neighbor
   A. kind
   B. thoughtful
   C. unfriendly
   D. handsome

14. the <u>old</u> house
   A. enormous
   B. young
   C. small
   D. new

15. the <u>tidy</u> garage
   A. messy
   B. neat
   C. small
   D. creepy

BE AWARE!
The format changed and so did the directions! Underline the key words in the directions.

Name: _Happy_ Date: _____

Lesson One: Vocabulary (cont.)

Directions: For items #16–22, read the sentences or phrases. Choose the word that best completes both sentences or phrases.

---

16. _____ the car near the door because it is raining.
    We were going to the _____ to play soccer.
    A. push
    B. park
    C. run
    D. start

17. Please _____ me the red pencil.
    Alicia burned her _____ baking cookies.
    A. throw
    B. eye
    C. hand
    D. fetch

18. Donald paid with a _____.
    The babysitter went to _____ on the baby.
    A. dollar
    B. credit card
    C. slap
    D. check

19. a string used to fasten a shoe
    a piece of needlework used to decorate clothes
    A. whip   C. cord
    B. lace   D. ribbon

20. a mixture of ingredients for baking
    a hitter in baseball
    A. striker   C. batter
    B. cake   D. starter

21. a course of study
    a citizen of a kingdom
    A. subject   C. social studies
    B. liege   D. queen

22. not heavy
    not dark
    A. easy   C. bright
    B. weak   D. light

> **BE SHARP!**
> #16–22 ask you to find the words that have more than one meaning.

> **BE READY!**
> #19–22 have different formats, but they are still asking for the word with multiple meanings.

Name: _____   Date: _____

Standardized Testing Grade 3 Answer Sheet

Unit Three: Mathematics   Lesson Two: Computation

1. Ⓐ Ⓑ Ⓒ Ⓓ   8. Ⓐ Ⓑ Ⓒ Ⓓ   15. Ⓐ Ⓑ Ⓒ Ⓓ   22. Ⓐ Ⓑ Ⓒ Ⓓ   29. Ⓐ Ⓑ Ⓒ Ⓓ
2. Ⓐ Ⓑ Ⓒ Ⓓ   9. Ⓐ Ⓑ Ⓒ Ⓓ   16. Ⓐ Ⓑ Ⓒ Ⓓ   23. Ⓐ Ⓑ Ⓒ Ⓓ   30. Ⓐ Ⓑ Ⓒ Ⓓ
3. Ⓐ Ⓑ Ⓒ Ⓓ   10. Ⓐ Ⓑ Ⓒ Ⓓ   17. Ⓐ Ⓑ Ⓒ Ⓓ   24. Ⓐ Ⓑ Ⓒ Ⓓ   31. Ⓐ Ⓑ Ⓒ Ⓓ
4. Ⓐ Ⓑ Ⓒ Ⓓ   11. Ⓐ Ⓑ Ⓒ Ⓓ   18. Ⓐ Ⓑ Ⓒ Ⓓ   25. Ⓐ Ⓑ Ⓒ Ⓓ   32. Ⓐ Ⓑ Ⓒ Ⓓ
5. Ⓐ Ⓑ Ⓒ Ⓓ   12. Ⓐ Ⓑ Ⓒ Ⓓ   19. Ⓐ Ⓑ Ⓒ Ⓓ   26. Ⓐ Ⓑ Ⓒ Ⓓ   33. Ⓐ Ⓑ Ⓒ Ⓓ
6. Ⓐ Ⓑ Ⓒ Ⓓ   13. Ⓐ Ⓑ Ⓒ Ⓓ   20. Ⓐ Ⓑ Ⓒ Ⓓ   27. Ⓐ Ⓑ Ⓒ Ⓓ   34. Ⓐ Ⓑ Ⓒ Ⓓ
7. Ⓐ Ⓑ Ⓒ Ⓓ   14. Ⓐ Ⓑ Ⓒ Ⓓ   21. Ⓐ Ⓑ Ⓒ Ⓓ   28. Ⓐ Ⓑ Ⓒ Ⓓ   35. Ⓐ Ⓑ Ⓒ Ⓓ

Unit Three: Mathematics   Lesson Three: Problem Solving and Reasoning

1. Ⓐ Ⓑ Ⓒ Ⓓ   7. Ⓐ Ⓑ Ⓒ Ⓓ   13. Ⓐ Ⓑ Ⓒ Ⓓ   19. Ⓐ Ⓑ Ⓒ Ⓓ   25. Ⓐ Ⓑ Ⓒ Ⓓ
2. Ⓐ Ⓑ Ⓒ Ⓓ   8. Ⓐ Ⓑ Ⓒ Ⓓ   14. Ⓐ Ⓑ Ⓒ Ⓓ   20. Ⓐ Ⓑ Ⓒ Ⓓ   26. Ⓐ Ⓑ Ⓒ Ⓓ
3. Ⓐ Ⓑ Ⓒ Ⓓ   9. Ⓐ Ⓑ Ⓒ Ⓓ   15. Ⓐ Ⓑ Ⓒ Ⓓ   21. Ⓐ Ⓑ Ⓒ Ⓓ   27. Ⓐ Ⓑ Ⓒ Ⓓ
4. Ⓐ Ⓑ Ⓒ Ⓓ   10. Ⓐ Ⓑ Ⓒ Ⓓ   16. Ⓐ Ⓑ Ⓒ Ⓓ   22. Ⓐ Ⓑ Ⓒ Ⓓ   28. Ⓐ Ⓑ Ⓒ Ⓓ
5. Ⓐ Ⓑ Ⓒ Ⓓ   11. Ⓐ Ⓑ Ⓒ Ⓓ   17. Ⓐ Ⓑ Ⓒ Ⓓ   23. Ⓐ Ⓑ Ⓒ Ⓓ   29. Ⓐ Ⓑ Ⓒ Ⓓ
6. Ⓐ Ⓑ Ⓒ Ⓓ   12. Ⓐ Ⓑ Ⓒ Ⓓ   18. Ⓐ Ⓑ Ⓒ Ⓓ   24. Ⓐ Ⓑ Ⓒ Ⓓ   30. Ⓐ Ⓑ Ⓒ Ⓓ

Unit Four: Science   Lesson One: Process and Inquiry

1. Ⓐ Ⓑ Ⓒ Ⓓ   5. Ⓐ Ⓑ Ⓒ Ⓓ   9. Ⓐ Ⓑ Ⓒ Ⓓ   13. Ⓐ Ⓑ Ⓒ Ⓓ   17. Ⓐ Ⓑ Ⓒ Ⓓ
2. Ⓐ Ⓑ Ⓒ Ⓓ   6. Ⓐ Ⓑ Ⓒ Ⓓ   10. Ⓐ Ⓑ Ⓒ Ⓓ   14. Ⓐ Ⓑ Ⓒ Ⓓ   18. Ⓐ Ⓑ Ⓒ Ⓓ
3. Ⓐ Ⓑ Ⓒ Ⓓ   7. Ⓐ Ⓑ Ⓒ Ⓓ   11. Ⓐ Ⓑ Ⓒ Ⓓ   15. Ⓐ Ⓑ Ⓒ Ⓓ   19. Ⓐ Ⓑ Ⓒ Ⓓ
4. Ⓐ Ⓑ Ⓒ Ⓓ   8. Ⓐ Ⓑ Ⓒ Ⓓ   12. Ⓐ Ⓑ Ⓒ Ⓓ   16. Ⓐ Ⓑ Ⓒ Ⓓ   20. Ⓐ Ⓑ Ⓒ Ⓓ

Unit Four: Science   Lesson Two: Concepts

1. Ⓐ Ⓑ Ⓒ Ⓓ   10. Ⓐ Ⓑ Ⓒ Ⓓ   19. Ⓐ Ⓑ Ⓒ Ⓓ   28. Ⓐ Ⓑ Ⓒ Ⓓ   37. Ⓐ Ⓑ Ⓒ Ⓓ
2. Ⓐ Ⓑ Ⓒ Ⓓ   11. Ⓐ Ⓑ Ⓒ Ⓓ   20. Ⓐ Ⓑ Ⓒ Ⓓ   29. Ⓐ Ⓑ Ⓒ Ⓓ   38. Ⓐ Ⓑ Ⓒ Ⓓ
3. Ⓐ Ⓑ Ⓒ Ⓓ   12. Ⓐ Ⓑ Ⓒ Ⓓ   21. Ⓐ Ⓑ Ⓒ Ⓓ   30. Ⓐ Ⓑ Ⓒ Ⓓ   39. Ⓐ Ⓑ Ⓒ Ⓓ
4. Ⓐ Ⓑ Ⓒ Ⓓ   13. Ⓐ Ⓑ Ⓒ Ⓓ   22. Ⓐ Ⓑ Ⓒ Ⓓ   31. Ⓐ Ⓑ Ⓒ Ⓓ   40. Ⓐ Ⓑ Ⓒ Ⓓ
5. Ⓐ Ⓑ Ⓒ Ⓓ   14. Ⓐ Ⓑ Ⓒ Ⓓ   23. Ⓐ Ⓑ Ⓒ Ⓓ   32. Ⓐ Ⓑ Ⓒ Ⓓ   41. Ⓐ Ⓑ Ⓒ Ⓓ
6. Ⓐ Ⓑ Ⓒ Ⓓ   15. Ⓐ Ⓑ Ⓒ Ⓓ   24. Ⓐ Ⓑ Ⓒ Ⓓ   33. Ⓐ Ⓑ Ⓒ Ⓓ   42. Ⓐ Ⓑ Ⓒ Ⓓ
7. Ⓐ Ⓑ Ⓒ Ⓓ   16. Ⓐ Ⓑ Ⓒ Ⓓ   25. Ⓐ Ⓑ Ⓒ Ⓓ   34. Ⓐ Ⓑ Ⓒ Ⓓ   43. Ⓐ Ⓑ Ⓒ Ⓓ
8. Ⓐ Ⓑ Ⓒ Ⓓ   17. Ⓐ Ⓑ Ⓒ Ⓓ   26. Ⓐ Ⓑ Ⓒ Ⓓ   35. Ⓐ Ⓑ Ⓒ Ⓓ   44. Ⓐ Ⓑ Ⓒ Ⓓ
9. Ⓐ Ⓑ Ⓒ Ⓓ   18. Ⓐ Ⓑ Ⓒ Ⓓ   27. Ⓐ Ⓑ Ⓒ Ⓓ   36. Ⓐ Ⓑ Ⓒ Ⓓ   45. Ⓐ Ⓑ Ⓒ Ⓓ

Name: _____   Date: _____

Standardized Testing Grade 3 Answer Sheet

Unit Five: Social Studies   **Lesson One: History and Culture**

1. Ⓐ Ⓑ Ⓒ Ⓓ	6. Ⓐ Ⓑ Ⓒ Ⓓ	11. Ⓐ Ⓑ Ⓒ Ⓓ	16. Ⓐ Ⓑ Ⓒ Ⓓ	21. Ⓐ Ⓑ Ⓒ Ⓓ
2. Ⓐ Ⓑ Ⓒ Ⓓ	7. Ⓐ Ⓑ Ⓒ Ⓓ	12. Ⓐ Ⓑ Ⓒ Ⓓ	17. Ⓐ Ⓑ Ⓒ Ⓓ	22. Ⓐ Ⓑ Ⓒ Ⓓ
3. Ⓐ Ⓑ Ⓒ Ⓓ	8. Ⓐ Ⓑ Ⓒ Ⓓ	13. Ⓐ Ⓑ Ⓒ Ⓓ	18. Ⓐ Ⓑ Ⓒ Ⓓ	23. Ⓐ Ⓑ Ⓒ Ⓓ
4. Ⓐ Ⓑ Ⓒ Ⓓ	9. Ⓐ Ⓑ Ⓒ Ⓓ	14. Ⓐ Ⓑ Ⓒ Ⓓ	19. Ⓐ Ⓑ Ⓒ Ⓓ	24. Ⓐ Ⓑ Ⓒ Ⓓ
5. Ⓐ Ⓑ Ⓒ Ⓓ	10. Ⓐ Ⓑ Ⓒ Ⓓ	15. Ⓐ Ⓑ Ⓒ Ⓓ	20. Ⓐ Ⓑ Ⓒ Ⓓ	25. Ⓐ Ⓑ Ⓒ Ⓓ

Unit Five: Social Studies   **Lesson Two: Civics, Government, and Economics**

1. Ⓐ Ⓑ Ⓒ Ⓓ	7. Ⓐ Ⓑ Ⓒ Ⓓ	13. Ⓐ Ⓑ Ⓒ Ⓓ	19. Ⓐ Ⓑ Ⓒ Ⓓ	25. Ⓐ Ⓑ Ⓒ Ⓓ
2. Ⓐ Ⓑ Ⓒ Ⓓ	8. Ⓐ Ⓑ Ⓒ Ⓓ	14. Ⓐ Ⓑ Ⓒ Ⓓ	20. Ⓐ Ⓑ Ⓒ Ⓓ	26. Ⓐ Ⓑ Ⓒ Ⓓ
3. Ⓐ Ⓑ Ⓒ Ⓓ	9. Ⓐ Ⓑ Ⓒ Ⓓ	15. Ⓐ Ⓑ Ⓒ Ⓓ	21. Ⓐ Ⓑ Ⓒ Ⓓ	27. Ⓐ Ⓑ Ⓒ Ⓓ
4. Ⓐ Ⓑ Ⓒ Ⓓ	10. Ⓐ Ⓑ Ⓒ Ⓓ	16. Ⓐ Ⓑ Ⓒ Ⓓ	22. Ⓐ Ⓑ Ⓒ Ⓓ	28. Ⓐ Ⓑ Ⓒ Ⓓ
5. Ⓐ Ⓑ Ⓒ Ⓓ	11. Ⓐ Ⓑ Ⓒ Ⓓ	17. Ⓐ Ⓑ Ⓒ Ⓓ	23. Ⓐ Ⓑ Ⓒ Ⓓ	29. Ⓐ Ⓑ Ⓒ Ⓓ
6. Ⓐ Ⓑ Ⓒ Ⓓ	12. Ⓐ Ⓑ Ⓒ Ⓓ	18. Ⓐ Ⓑ Ⓒ Ⓓ	24. Ⓐ Ⓑ Ⓒ Ⓓ	30. Ⓐ Ⓑ Ⓒ Ⓓ

Unit Five: Social Studies   **Lesson Three: Geography**

1. Ⓐ Ⓑ Ⓒ Ⓓ	8. Ⓐ Ⓑ Ⓒ Ⓓ	15. Ⓐ Ⓑ Ⓒ Ⓓ	22. Ⓐ Ⓑ Ⓒ Ⓓ	29. Ⓐ Ⓑ Ⓒ Ⓓ
2. Ⓐ Ⓑ Ⓒ Ⓓ	9. Ⓐ Ⓑ Ⓒ Ⓓ	16. Ⓐ Ⓑ Ⓒ Ⓓ	23. Ⓐ Ⓑ Ⓒ Ⓓ	30. Ⓐ Ⓑ Ⓒ Ⓓ
3. Ⓐ Ⓑ Ⓒ Ⓓ	10. Ⓐ Ⓑ Ⓒ Ⓓ	17. Ⓐ Ⓑ Ⓒ Ⓓ	24. Ⓐ Ⓑ Ⓒ Ⓓ	31. Ⓐ Ⓑ Ⓒ Ⓓ
4. Ⓐ Ⓑ Ⓒ Ⓓ	11. Ⓐ Ⓑ Ⓒ Ⓓ	18. Ⓐ Ⓑ Ⓒ Ⓓ	25. Ⓐ Ⓑ Ⓒ Ⓓ	32. Ⓐ Ⓑ Ⓒ Ⓓ
5. Ⓐ Ⓑ Ⓒ Ⓓ	12. Ⓐ Ⓑ Ⓒ Ⓓ	19. Ⓐ Ⓑ Ⓒ Ⓓ	26. Ⓐ Ⓑ Ⓒ Ⓓ	33. Ⓐ Ⓑ Ⓒ Ⓓ
6. Ⓐ Ⓑ Ⓒ Ⓓ	13. Ⓐ Ⓑ Ⓒ Ⓓ	20. Ⓐ Ⓑ Ⓒ Ⓓ	27. Ⓐ Ⓑ Ⓒ Ⓓ	34. Ⓐ Ⓑ Ⓒ Ⓓ
7. Ⓐ Ⓑ Ⓒ Ⓓ	14. Ⓐ Ⓑ Ⓒ Ⓓ	21. Ⓐ Ⓑ Ⓒ Ⓓ	28. Ⓐ Ⓑ Ⓒ Ⓓ	35. Ⓐ Ⓑ Ⓒ Ⓓ

Standardized Testing Grade 3 Answer Key

School:

Teacher:

Female ○   Male ○

Birth Date

Month	Day	Year
Jan ○	⓪ ⓪	⓪ ⓪
Feb ○	① ①	① ①
Mar ○	② ②	② ②
Apr ○	③ ③	③ ③
May ○	④	④ ④
Jun ○	⑤	⑤ ⑤
Jul ○	⑥	⑥ ⑥
Aug ○	⑦	⑦ ⑦
Sep ○	⑧	⑧ ⑧
Oct ○	⑨	⑨ ⑨
Nov ○		
Dec ○		

Grade ③ ④ ⑤ ⑥ ⑦ ⑧

Student Name

Last — First — MI

(Name grid with circles and letters A–Z for each column)

Unit One: Reading   Lesson One: Vocabulary

1. Ⓐ **Ⓑ** Ⓒ Ⓓ   9. **Ⓐ** Ⓑ Ⓒ Ⓓ   17. Ⓐ Ⓑ **Ⓒ** Ⓓ   25. Ⓐ Ⓑ **Ⓒ** Ⓓ   33. Ⓐ Ⓑ Ⓒ **Ⓓ**
2. **Ⓐ** Ⓑ Ⓒ Ⓓ   10. Ⓐ Ⓑ **Ⓒ** Ⓓ   18. Ⓐ Ⓑ Ⓒ **Ⓓ**   26. Ⓐ **Ⓑ** Ⓒ Ⓓ   34. Ⓐ Ⓑ **Ⓒ** Ⓓ
3. Ⓐ Ⓑ Ⓒ **Ⓓ**   11. Ⓐ **Ⓑ** Ⓒ Ⓓ   19. Ⓐ **Ⓑ** Ⓒ Ⓓ   27. Ⓐ Ⓑ **Ⓒ** Ⓓ   35. Ⓐ **Ⓑ** Ⓒ Ⓓ
4. **Ⓐ** Ⓑ Ⓒ Ⓓ   12. Ⓐ Ⓑ **Ⓒ** Ⓓ   20. Ⓐ Ⓑ **Ⓒ** Ⓓ   28. **Ⓐ** Ⓑ Ⓒ Ⓓ   36. Ⓐ **Ⓑ** Ⓒ Ⓓ
5. Ⓐ Ⓑ **Ⓒ** Ⓓ   13. Ⓐ Ⓑ **Ⓒ** Ⓓ   21. **Ⓐ** Ⓑ Ⓒ Ⓓ   29. Ⓐ Ⓑ Ⓒ **Ⓓ**   37. Ⓐ Ⓑ **Ⓒ** Ⓓ
6. Ⓐ **Ⓑ** Ⓒ Ⓓ   14. Ⓐ Ⓑ Ⓒ **Ⓓ**   22. Ⓐ Ⓑ Ⓒ **Ⓓ**   30. Ⓐ **Ⓑ** Ⓒ Ⓓ   38. Ⓐ **Ⓑ** Ⓒ Ⓓ
7. **Ⓐ** Ⓑ Ⓒ Ⓓ   15. **Ⓐ** Ⓑ Ⓒ Ⓓ   23. Ⓐ **Ⓑ** Ⓒ Ⓓ   31. Ⓐ **Ⓑ** Ⓒ Ⓓ   39. Ⓐ Ⓑ **Ⓒ** Ⓓ
8. Ⓐ Ⓑ Ⓒ **Ⓓ**   16. Ⓐ **Ⓑ** Ⓒ Ⓓ   24. **Ⓐ** Ⓑ Ⓒ Ⓓ   32. Ⓐ **Ⓑ** Ⓒ Ⓓ   40. **Ⓐ** Ⓑ Ⓒ Ⓓ

Standardized Testing Grade 3 Answer Key

Unit One: Reading — Lesson Two: Word Analysis

#	Ans	#	Ans	#	Ans	#	Ans	#	Ans
1	A	7	C	13	C	19	C	25	A
2	C	8	A	14	A	20	D	26	B
3	C	9	C	15	C	21	B		
4	B	10	B	16	C	22	B		
5	A	11	C	17	B	23	A		
6	B	12	B	18	A	24	B		

Unit One: Reading — Lesson Three: Reading Comprehension

#	Ans	#	Ans	#	Ans	#	Ans	#	Ans
1	B	6	C	11	D	16	B	21	C
2	D	7	B	12	A	17	C	22	C
3	D	8	D	13	A	18	A	23	D
4	A	9	A	14	B	19	C	24	A
5	C	10	C	15	A	20	A	25	C

Unit Two: Language — Lesson One: Mechanics

#	Ans	#	Ans	#	Ans	#	Ans	#	Ans
1	C	16	A	31	C	46	D	61	A
2	A	17	A	32	B	47	B	62	C
3	C	18	B	33	B	48	C	63	C
4	D	19	A	34	A	49	A	64	A
5	A	20	B	35	A	50	B	65	B
6	C	21	C	36	B	51	B	66	C
7	A	22	B	37	B	52	C	67	B
8	B	23	C	38	C	53	A	68	D
9	B	24	B	39	A	54	B	69	C
10	C	25	A	40	B	55	A	70	B
11	C	26	A	41	A	56	A	71	A
12	C	27	B	42	B	57	D	72	C
13	A	28	D	43	C	58	B	73	B
14	D	29	C	44	A	59	C	74	D
15	B	30	A	45	B	60	B	75	C

Standardized Testing Grade 3 Answer Key

Unit Two: Language   **Lesson Two: Expression**

1. C	11. B	21. B	31. D	41. D
2. A	12. B	22. B	32. B	42. B
3. B	13. B	23. A	33. D	43. D
4. A	14. A	24. A	34. A	44. C
5. C	15. B	25. A	35. A	45. A
6. A	16. C	26. C	36. A	46. D
7. C	17. A	27. A	37. C	47. A
8. A	18. C	28. A	38. A	48. A
9. D	19. D	29. C	39. C	49. C
10. A	20. C	30. C	40. D	50. A

Unit Two: Language   **Lesson Three: Information Skills**

1. B	9. D	17. C	25. B	33. D
2. B	10. D	18. B	26. D	34. A
3. A	11. C	19. D	27. C	35. B
4. B	12. D	20. A	28. A	36. C
5. B	13. A	21. D	29. A	37. D
6. C	14. C	22. C	30. C	38. B
7. B	15. D	23. A	31. B	39. C
8. A	16. A	24. B	32. C	40. A

Unit Three: Mathematics   **Lesson One: Concepts**

1. B	11. D	21. D	31. C	41. D
2. D	12. B	22. B	32. C	42. A
3. C	13. B	23. B	33. A	43. B
4. B	14. B	24. B	34. D	44. A
5. B	15. D	25. C	35. D	45. B
6. C	16. A	26. C	36. B	46. D
7. B	17. A	27. D	37. C	47. C
8. C	18. C	28. C	38. C	48. A
9. A	19. B	29. A	39. A	49. A
10. B	20. B	30. C	40. C	50. B

Standardized Testing Grade 3 Answer Key

Unit Three: Mathematics   Lesson Two: Computation

1. A	8. B	15. C	22. B	29. D
2. D	9. C	16. A	23. B	30. C
3. B	10. A	17. A	24. A	31. C
4. A	11. A	18. C	25. C	32. A
5. C	12. C	19. D	26. D	33. B
6. C	13. B	20. B	27. A	34. C
7. C	14. A	21. C	28. A	35. C

Unit Three: Mathematics   Lesson Three: Problem Solving and Reasoning

1. C	7. A	13. D	19. D	25. C
2. D	8. C	14. A	20. C	26. B
3. B	9. A	15. D	21. B	27. B
4. A	10. B	16. B	22. A	28. A
5. D	11. D	17. C	23. C	29. A
6. B	12. C	18. B	24. B	30. A

Unit Four: Science   Lesson One: Process and Inquiry

1. A	5. C	9. D	13. D	17. D
2. C	6. B	10. B	14. B	18. B
3. B	7. D	11. D	15. A	19. A
4. D	8. A	12. A	16. C	20. C

Unit Four: Science   Lesson Two: Concepts

1. B	10. A	19. B	28. C	37. B
2. C	11. D	20. A	29. A	38. A
3. B	12. D	21. B	30. B	39. C
4. A	13. B	22. D	31. B	40. D
5. D	14. C	23. A	32. A	41. C
6. C	15. A	24. D	33. A	42. C
7. D	16. A	25. B	34. C	43. C
8. C	17. A	26. C	35. C	44. C
9. B	18. A	27. A	36. C	45. C